BACK IN TIME

GB ISBN 90 288 2977 6

© 1984 European Library – Zaltbommel/The Netherlands

Third edition, 1998: reprint of the original edition of 1984.

CW00433365

Glasgow
in old picture postcards

by Innes Macleod

European Library ZALTBOMMEL/THE NETHERLANDS

INTRODUCTION

Glasgow in the 1900s was one of the great cities of the British Empire, large enough and wealthy enough to be a self-sufficient regional and even national centre for the production and sale of high art and popular culture. It was also a place of contrasts between at one end of the social scale the spectacular personal wealth and very conspicuous expenditure of successful industrialists and capitalists in their opulent piles and palaces, and the (in comparison) seeming mediocrity of the lives of the vast mass of the population. Yet these 'working classes' included not only possibly the most skilled and disciplined and hard-working but also, in the context of the period, many of the most prosperous and best housed industrial workers in the British Isles. The men living in Glasgow in 1901 and working in shipbuilding, or in the iron and steel industry (2,818 in Pig Iron Manufacture Blast Furnaces, 1,116 in Puddling Furnaces and Rolling Mills, and 2,372 in Steel Smelting and Founding) were truly an elite work force. And the men in engineering and machine making thought of themselves in the same way as the best there was, the 1,002 patternmakers, 6,377 ironfounders, 749 brassfounders, 4,953 blacksmiths and strikers, 8,709 erectors, fitters and turners, 1,358 brass finishers, 533 coppersmiths, 1,810 metal machinists, 3,475 boiler makers and 5,656 others. In striking contrast the old cotton textile industry still employed 1,093 men and 5,828 women, and in what seemed a promising new development 1,945 men were employed in the manufacture of electrical apparatus. In essence this was a confident city, assured of success, optimistic, bubbling over with energy and a market for consumer goods of all kinds.

As the postcards suggest Glasgow was a spectacularly busy city, bustling, brassy, overcrowded, although by 1901 it had long since burst out of its mediaeval boundaries, taking over Gorbals as far back as 1846, and Govanhill, Crosshill, Maryhill, Hillhead and Pollokshields as recently as 1891. The 1901 population of Glasgow was 761,709 (Govan with 76,350 and Partick with 54,281 remained outside Glasgow until 1912).

Edwardian Glasgow was an important art market. By and large wealthy collectors purchased paintings, and the people bought postcards which in terms of the significance they had for large numbers of people were a far more important art form and certainly provided far more pleasure and enjoyment and laughter than the sometimes weird high art of the 'West End'. And Glasgow postcard publishers and manufacturers, in particular the Art Publishing Company and Miller and Lang, created a whole 'Glasgow School of Postcards' whose special strength lay in humourous cards.

This emphasis is distinctly surprising given the presence in Glasgow of one of the most distinguished photographic firms in Scotland, T. and R. Annan and Sons, whose collection of topographical prints provided an invaluable panorama of nineteenth century and Edwardian Glasgow. Thomas Annan, commissioned by the Glasgow Improvement Trust and by the University of Glasgow, had taken a marvellous series of photographs of the old city in the late 1860s and the 1870s, and his successors after his death in 1887 had continued and expanded their photographic business in Sauchiehall Street. It might have been expected that Glasgow firms would have effectively monopolised the manufacture and sale of pictorial postcards incorporating photographs of Glasgow scenes. However T. and R. Annan and Sons (unlike, for example,

Valentine of Dundee) did not move in this direction and instead it was two Edingburgh firms, J.A. McCulloch and William Ritchie and Sons, who published the most important cards with Glasgow topographical scenes in the 1900s.

John A. McCulloch, wholesale stationer, paper merchant, lithographic and letterpress printer, of 70 Montgomery Street, Edinburgh, and later of Hillside Printing Works, Gorgie, published the Caledonia Series of postcards which included a number with the old and by then classical Annan photographs. William Ritchie and Sons, wholesale stationers and fancy good merchants, of Elder Street, Edinburgh, published the excellent quality Reliable Series, which also included old photographs. They had a Glasgow base (before the postcard boom started) at the Victoria Chambers, 142 West Nile Street, later in the Grosvenor Buildings, 68 Gordon Street, and then about 1909-10 at Morrison's Court, 108 Argyle Street. Another Edinburgh publisher whose stock included Glasgow cards was William Nimmo and Company of 46 Constitution Street and 30,31,32 Quality Street.

The most famous Glasgow firm of pictorial postcard manufacturers, Miller and Lang, was listed in the Glasgow Post Office Directory for 1901-02 as 'fancy stationery and Christmas card manufacturers and art publishers' of 34 Paternoster Row, London and 5 and 7 Robertson Lane, Glasgow, but their Darnley Street factory, built in 1901 with additions in 1903, became their principal centre about this time. The Art Publishing Company, first listed in the Glasgow Post Office Directory in 1905-06, was based at 48 King Street, City (that is in 'Old Glasgow' itself). The great strength of both these firms lay in the sheer excellence of the drawings and sketches prepared by their illustrators and artists (almost all anonymous figures) and in the quality and delicacy of the colouring applied to their cards. It is also fair to say that their humour was characterised by a delicacy and wholesomeness which makes a sharp contrast with the 'seaside slapstick' style associated with many comic postcards. Of course, there are exceptions to this general assessment of their work and anyway taste in these matters does vary considerably from generation to generation and from individual to individual.

Another interesting Glasgow postcard manufacturer was F. Bauermeister, 'foreign bookseller and publisher', of 49 Gordon Street, who produced rather distinguished cards with a distinctly Germanic flavour although dealing with local Glasgow topics.

Other Glasgow publishers and/or manufacturers of postcards in the Edwardian era variously listed in the Post Office Directories included William Ralston, the photographer, of 259 Sauchiehall Street; William Collins Sons and Company Ltd., Herriot Hill Works, 139-153 Stirling Road; W. and A.K. Johnston Ltd., Castle Chambers, 55 West Regent Street; Boots, Cash Chemists, 101 Sauchiehall Street; William Holmes and Company, 9 Mitchell Lane; Thomson Brown and Company, Eclipse Works, 29/39 Surrey Street; Valentine and Sons (of Dundee), 19 Waterloo Street, and later of 27 Jamaica Street; John Miller, 116 Renfield Street; E. Murray and Company, 53 Bothwell Street, and later of 52-56 Darnley Street; A. Gray, 43 Renfield Street; John Gardiner, 28 Findlay Street; Newman Brothers, 19 Howard Street; The Rotary Photographic Company, 142 Queen Street; Forrest and Son, 11-25 Bishop Street, Anderston Cross; and W. Watson, 133 High Street. In addition the Willesden Chrome Printing Company of London was listed as using Brown,

Primrose and Smith, 68 Gordon Street, as their local agents. Another interesting aspect of the postcard industry is recalled in the name of David Campbell and Sons of 100 West Campbell Street who were listed in the 1907-08 Directory as 'publishers and manufacturers of postcards display holders and stands'.

The cards used for this collection, the vast majority published from about 1902 to 1907, have been arranged in six sections. They include examples of the work of many of these Edinburgh and Glasgow publishers. 1-33 is planned to show how people in Edwardian Glasgow used postcards and to suggest something of the range of subjects and ideas to be found in them. 34-51 is essentially an 'Old Glasgow' section with examples from the Caledonia Series and the Reliable Series using old photographs of the nineteenth century city.

52-98 is in the main a conventional topographical section dealing with Glasgow in the 1900s. As a number of excellent books of photographs of buildings of architectural distinction in Victorian and Edwardian Glasgow have been published in recent years, this particular aspect has not been developed here to any great extent. Cards showing the people of Glasgow (Scots, Irish, Italians, Russian and Polish Jews) in close-up detail in the streets or at work are very scarce; unfortunately this type of card, so useful to illustrate city life in, for example, Berlin, does not seem to have been popular in Glasgow.

99-118 deals with the River Clyde, shipping, Glasgow folk on holiday 'Doon th' Watter' en masse and on the railways. 119-131 presents a little of the marvellous gallery of popular culture experienced through postcards of the 1901 and 1911 Exhibitions. And 132-138 has a sample of the range of lively, charming, delightfully amusing and 'clean fun' in Miller and Lang and Art Publishing Company cards.

Dating postcards is not quite as straightforward as the notes on each card might seem to suggest. Undivided backs are likely to have been published before 1902. Postmarks, where present, prove only that the card must have been manufactured before that date. Neither fact necessarily establishes when the pictorial element, whether from a photograph or from the hand of an artist/illustrator, was made. The McCulloch Caledonia Series using photographs of 34 to 36 years earlier is the obvious example; when the Reliable Series photographs were taken is much more difficult.

The presence or absence of tramlines and of horse-drawn or electric trams can provide useful dating clues. The tramway lines, laid by the Corporation and leased to the Glasgow Tramways and Omnibus Company, were first used by horse-drawn trams on a route in 1872. To keep a more complex story to essentials, the Corporation took over the by then extensive system in 1894. A trial electric route was opened in 1898 and electrification of the whole system was completed to coincide with the opening of the 1901 International Exhibition.

Postcards and photographs of the 1901 Exhibition leave the impression of a brilliantly managed presentation by 'Glasgow Limited' confirming Glasgow's international and imperial status as a centre of industry and commerce. The well-dressed crowds suggest the presence in Glasgow of a large and affluent 'middling class', just as street scenes of the period suggest that the 'workers' were well-paid and above all employed. In contrast the photographs of 1868-1877 suggest a vast morass of depravity and desperate poverty. These almost equally illustrate some of the problems, as well as the advantages, in using pictorial material as evidence, because in neither case is this a wholly adequate view of the 'new' or the 'old' Glasgow. It is all too easy merely to fit photographs into preconceived stereotypes which just because they bring the subjects to life so well can further oversimplify and distort realities.

So some care is necessary in using postcards to illustrate even already generally statistically established points. They are particularly interesting evidence in any attempt to assess the quality of life of any group of people in a street or a ward or a city, however difficult or almost impossible this may be. On the one hand postcards of Edwardian Glasgow show it as a very formal, indeed a stuffy world of overdressed adults and even more overdressed children whether in parks or shops or street scenes. But in any 'Happiness Index' Edwardian Glasgow on postcard evidence would be likely to score high marks, for this does seem to be a place full of vitality and optimism and youthful exuberance, brassy and vulgar perhaps but outgoing and businesslike and purposeful. This is probably all true, and yet, and yet... is this an adequate view? For it has to be said that there is a whole underworld of poverty and crime and prostitution and religious bigotry largely ignored in this material. This is hardly surprising, for postcards full of gloom and grime and girning were not likely to be bestsellers – the Caledonia Series Annan photographs may well have been seen in the 1900s as evidence of the 'bad old days' to compare with the great improvements that had taken place since then, rather than as evidence to encourage study of housing and social problems in the contemporary world.

One essential tool for examining postcards is a magnifying glass. This makes it possible to see the vignettes of groups of people and the details of shop fronts and advertisements which are so rewarding and also to detect the 'faking' or 'improvements' added to photographers by postcard manufacturers.

It is worthwhile remembering also that these are very human documents. The gossipy family messages, the data scribbled for collectors and transport enthusiasts, and the everyday mundane practical wants and needs expressed on the back of the cards are worth reading and recording. They are in themselves also evidence of attitudes and expectations whether in terms of home and family, work and holidays, or of what was perceived as amusing and funny. The last is often far more important than anything else.

We are grateful for the helpful cooperation received and for permission to reproduce postcards and photographs from:
The People's Palace: 1, 5, 32, 34, 35, 36, 38, 44, 46, 47, 48, 49, 50, 51, 72, 101, 118, 119, and 120.
The Mitchell Library: 18, 24, and 124.
T. and R. Annan and Sons: 39, 42, 43, 57, 83, 117, and 131.
The University Library, University of Glasgow: 121, 122, and 123.
The National Trust for Scotland: 104 and 108.

1. Greetings from Glasgow, or 39 girls and 1 man in letters set against a very George Gilbert Scott pickle of pinnacles and spires, plus coat of arms and motto. The odd man out, rather incongruously in clerical garb, is at the top of the 'A'. In a Gilbertian world the modest maidens with the remarkable coiffures and the fashionable hats would have been the daughters of Glasgow councillors. In reality the same girls, more or less, can be encountered in RHYL or EASTBOURNE and were more likely to have been from the London chorus line of 'Our Miss Gibbs' or 'The Arcadians'. They could have been recruited, had this been a local card, from the ranks of the actresses (81 in Glasgow, 10 in Govan and 1 in Partick) and the musicians and music teachers and singers (525 in Glasgow, 32 in Govan and 44 in Partick) listed in the 1901 Census. A lovely brassy, vulgar Edwardian postcard, thoroughly part of the period, and at the same time superbly and cleverly designed and executed.

Glasgow.

Sauchiehall Street, Glasgow.

[handwritten postcard message: Friday morning. Dear Maggie, I find that by working a little later to-morrow night I can get away as usual on (to-morrow) Saturday, so I will take a run down. Love to all from ... Smith. I will try to be in Greenock about 4 p.m., but if not, will be certain by 5 p.m. & hope you harn't to soon ... at that time as]

2. An 'undivided back' postcard with the picture and the message on one side and the name and address taking the whole of the other. Post Office regulations stipulating this format were altered early in 1902 and 'divided backs' with the picture on one side and the message on one half of the reverse became general thereafter, although older cards were still, as here, used until stocks were exhausted. Posted on a Friday in 1903 to Miss (Maggie) Macpherson of Greenock (West), this is a good example of how postcards were used before the age of the telephone to confirm or cancel or alter appointments and social engagements. The Post Office provided a rapid and reliable same or next day delivery service for ½d. In spite of the small size of the picture the definition is excellent, showing clearly the electric tram car and tram lines and the lettering on the shop fronts. Electric trams generally date from 1901, so this photograph of Sauchiehall Street belongs to 1901 or 1902.

Handwritten postcard text (as visible on the card):

April. 29th 1901.

Clayton Road ... How sweet
Jesmond. of you to
send me such
a dear tiny letter
this morning. I
did laugh when
I saw the size.
I hope Prince is
alright again, he
is rather an un-
fortunate little
dog isn't he dear?

University. to hear about poor Mrs Brown. Glasgow. I was very sorry
are you coming back darling? I am looking greatly forward
to seeing you again — I hope you will like this Postcard.
With heaps of love to dear mother, dear Niss Browing & espec...

3. An undivided back card with an (in the original) coloured picture of the University from the south-east. Dated 29 April 1901 and sent to Miss Vivian Wheater at Burford Bridge Hotel near Dorking. The most interesting cards are those with crowded, indeed densely crammed, handwriting and this is a typically charming, light, affectionate message. Note the phrase 'I hope you will like this postcard', so common at this time when collecting was well on the way to becoming a major leisure interest. Neither publisher nor photographer is mentioned, but the card was quite probably produced locally. The 1901 Census for Glasgow, Govan and Partick lists 228, 11 and 20 men and 267, 9 and 12 women employed as photographers.

GLASGOW.

RELIABLE [WR&S] SERIES 272.

4. A lively composite card of the type printed as a decorative object for collectors and one of thousands published in the Reliable Series by the Edinburgh firm of William Ritchie and Sons which specialised in topographical subjects. The original is very brightly coloured with a rich pattern of vividly pink bell-shaped flowers and green stems, probably bell-heather or Erica Cinerea, embracing the miniature photographs which are set into a black background. Prussia and Saxony had a thriving export trade in printing cards coloured by hand and by lithographic processes, and this example was chromotyped in Saxony. The pictures, clockwise from the top centre, show Great Western Road, Argyle Street, the Sculpture Court in the Kelvingrove Art Gallery, Jamaica Bridge, George Square and Sauchiehall Street.

5. A marvellously decorative card coloured in delicate creamy blues and purples. No doubt more often than not the card was frae yin ye kent, but if ye didna you had 20,266 males and 19,152 females in Springburn in 1901 to choose from. Most of them sent or received postcards at some time in their lives, as between 1900 and 1914 the Post Office delivered annually between 500 and 880 million cards in Great Britain. If 600 million were posted in 1903, how many were posted in Glasgow? At a guess 5 or 6 or 7 million, and vast numbers of these went merely from one ward of the city to another, from Springburn to Maryhill or Cowlairs or Anderston or Gorbals, and they flowed back in from the holiday hot spots of Dunoon and Rothesay and from all over the world from Pago Pago to Auchtermuchty.

6. Plagues of postcards indeed, and a vast source of ideas and information about Glasgow and its people, just as the cards themselves were a powerful medium for spreading and reinforcing popular attitudes and prejudices. Written messages are usually light gossip, but some do convey a certain minor malice aforethought, as in the pointed identifications in this National Series card by Miller and Lang of Glasgow posted on 15 July 1905. The domineering wife with red hair and hat and skirt and some social pretensions is followed by her hen-pecked husband with their brood of seven children. The poor chap is perhaps one of the vast army of 12,850 commercial and business clerks or one of the 1,662 railway clerks in Glasgow in 1901. (Govan and Partick had 948 and 867 of the former and 57 and 95 of the latter.)

7. Given the pressures of overcrowding and large families, and there were 5,393 family units of 9 in Glasgow in 1901, postcards dealing with marital disharmony and family problems were very popular. This marvellous Art Publishing Company of Glasgow card, posted in Bridge of Weir on 5 July 1905, takes the more optimistic view of the position of the happy although downtrodden male. Beautifully drawn, hilarious, and at the same time very informative on dress and footwear. As the writer of the postcard says: 'Isnt it delightful?'

HOW TO BE HAPPY THO' MARRIED

Isnt it delightful?

When father said 'rise' we all rose.

339

8. Miller and Lang produced very witty and socially relevant cards, including the 'Father said turn' and the 'Father said rise' series. These may have been pictures of conditions in holiday lodgings, or they may be seen as describing, even while exaggerating, a real situation in contemporary Glasgow since there were 2,797 family units of 10 in 1901, and 1,172 of these were in houses with only two rooms. One criticism might be that the children in those circumstances would not, in fact, be dressed so neatly in nightgowns. As the writer of the card, posted in 1906, says in the message on the reverse side: 'Be good to the children.'

9. A Christmas card posted in 1903 to Mrs. Henderson of Dixon Avenue. A beautiful card printed in Prussia and published by Stewart and Woolf of London. The original in green and orange-pink and yellow and silver set against a black ground is rather like an illuminated initial in a mediaeval manuscript. Note the two small children, the seven candles on a Christmas tree behind, and the soulful and rather dishy but angelic lady with a pearl necklace, a richly theatrical costume, and long woolly tresses decorated with leaves and a silver clasp, topped off with a halo. Posted on the afternoon of 24 December for delivery on Christmas Day.

10. Postcards were very generally used as greetings cards for Christmas, New Year, Easter, St. Patrick's Day, for birthdays, and as Valentine cards. Christmas cards were prone to be filled with cherubs and angels, but were quite often merely everyday cards utilised for seasonal good wishes. This Miller and Lang card posted in 1907 has 'With best Wishes for a Merry Christmas from' stamped on the back so that the sender has only to add his or her name. Sent to a farm near Glenbuchat in Aberdeenshire no doubt the postcard was carefully chosen to suit the recipient, and is, of course, very typical of the good-natured ribaldry found in so many Scottish cards of the period.

11. Celebrities from the world of music hall and repertory theatre and men and women in public life from W.E. Gladstone to William Morris were popular subjects for postcards. Wee Macgreegor (not Macgregor, and it sounds very different) was one of the great Scottish folk heroes, as well known in his day as Wee Willie Winkie and Oor Wullie. He appeared in stories in the Glasgow vernacular by J.J. Bell of the Glasgow Evening News. A collection published in November 1902, illustrated by John Hassall, sold vast numbers of copies. An edition was published in New York in 1903. Wee Macgreegor toffees and lemonades and postcards followed quickly on the initial success. This card was posted in Glasgow on 4 March 1903. The drawing is effective perhaps just because it is realistic and restrained, interestingly not tartan tosh, and with the only colour red for his socks and scarf and the bob on his bonnet.

"WEE MACGREEGOR."

Visit of the Prince & Princess of Wales to Glasgow, April 23rd 1907.

12. Glasgow as the patriotic British imperial city welcoming the Prince and Princess of Wales, later George V and Queen Mary, on 23 April 1907. Notice the Union Jacks out in plenty. Postcards with royals and the innumerable distant relations of Queen Victoria and most of the royal families of Europe, however obscure, were collected with as much enthusiasm as those of film stars in the 1930s and 1940s. Posted in Glasgow in 1907 to Mr. Willie Bell of Cookston, Co. Tyrone and full of good advice in the message on the reverse side. 'This is one of the principal streets they went through. It was beautiful decorated. I hope you are enjoying yourself and see and dont be flirting take my advice.'

13. Perhaps following in the tradition of the carte-de-visit, it was quite normal in the 1900s to send photographic souvenirs to friends in the form of postcards. This was partly because photographers used 'postcard paper', that is photographic paper with the postcard details already printed on the reverse side. Thousands of Glasgow folk were included in records of this type and it is important for family history archives that these should be collected, essentially if possible with details on the back of the people concerned. Costume and dress is particularly good. Note here the elaborate detail, including jewellery, round necks and shoulders. These young ladies may have been three of the 2,573 female schoolmasters and teachers in Glasgow in 1901 (225 in Govan and 234 in Partick), or among the 4,959 female commercial and business clerks (370 in Govan and 335 in Partick).

14. To the woods with an unidentified group, but very probably a Sunday School Teachers' outing. A lovely atmospheric card, with a professionally assembled group photograph in which all 18 persons are clearly visible (just possibly someone behind the lady with the polka dot blouse sitting on the rock in the centre). Excellent costume details, and typically Edwardian in the manner in which nearly everyone is so over-dressed for out-of-doors. What discomfort for the sake of propriety and convention! And it was considered almost sinful and certainly injurious to health to be without a hat. This, of course, was a fortunate generation for most of the young ladies would have been able to acquire husbands; it was very different post 1914-1918 and the Western front.

15. Glasgow Thornhill and District Friendly and Benevolent Association party on an outing to Morton Castle, Dumfries-shire, 15 July 1918. Note the tremendous contrast in male and female attire with the details in the previous postcard of some 15 years earlier. Glasgow was a melting-pot for thousands of Irish men and women and for Highlanders from the north and west of Scotland, but also for many families from Ayrshire, Wigtownshire, the Stewartry of Kirkcudbright and Dumfries-shire. Many groups were formed in Glasgow of exiles from Skye, Islay, Galloway, Caithness, indeed from all over the rest of Scotland, and quite commonly these took the form of Friendly Societies to help to look after the poor and destitute in Glasgow whose roots were in other parts of Scotland.

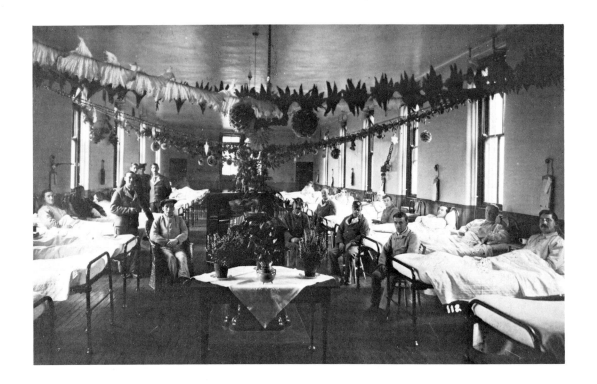

16. Stobhill, 20 January 1918. The enthusiasm for postcards of the years before 1914 was never quite recaptured again, and undoubtedly quality suffered with the loss of German printing facilities. Vast numbers of postcards were still produced during the war years as part of the propaganda machine, but the hospital and cemetery scenes are more evocative than most obviously patriotic material. The ward here, with the rather sad attempts at decoration, is one of the thousands in France and Great Britain in a war that had gone badly wrong.

17. Glaswegians. Female domestic servants, including cooks, totalled 16,241 in Glasgow in 1901, with 760 more in Govan and 1,674 in Partick. Another 577, 22, and 2 respectively worked in hotels, lodging and eating houses in Glasgow, Govan and Partick. A Miller and Lang National Series card posted in Dunoon in 1904 to a friend in Paisley Road, Glasgow. 'Dear Lizzie, I hope this wont happen if you visit some of the camps. I hope you enjoy your holidays. Tell all we were asking for them. Daft Nan.' A very nice message, and a reminder of the British enthusiasm for uniforms and military bands and one-sided wars and local militias before 1914.

169

"Oh My Dear Liz."

OUR CLOSE 10 P.M.

18. Glaswegians. A most evocative signed sketch, dated 1904, and published by F. Bauermeister in Glasgow. It might also have had as a title 'the queue', so congested were tenement buildings and closes. A scene familiar to generations of Glasgow folk, although judging by the dress this is a rather properous tenement area. No wall tiles, however, which is a pity as this would have given more information on locale. Bauermeister cards seem to be quite different in style from the Miller and Lang and the Art Publishing Company publications, and rather more refined and elegant productions.

19. Glaswegians. Another Bauermeister postcard, again signed, and posted on 10 June 1907. A charming drawing, reminiscent of the great Alfred Concanen music sheet covers satirising the aesthetic movement in the 1880s. Possibly an instantly recognisable figure in Glasgow in the 1900s. The card is lined and shaded entirely in red. The daft-looking gowk is clearly affluent, possibly a doctor (550 physicians, surgeons and general practitioners in Glasgow in 1901), a lawyer (457 advocates and solicitors in Glasgow), a dentist (232), or with a higher probability factor a dealer in works of art (34 in Glasgow in 1901, of whom 12 are employers, 11 are working for employers, and 11 are working on their own account).

I WORSHIP THE GROUND YOU WALK ON

When a man's single he lives at his ease.

20. Glaswegians. A Miller and Lang National Series card, identified on the reverse side as 'Harold', and instantly therefore Harold from Hillhead – which goes with the wall bookcase and the elegant fireplace and table setting. Perhaps one of the 150 authors, editors and journalists in Glasgow in 1901, or a publisher and bookseller (319 in Glasgow, including 55 employers and 29 working on their own account), or a printer (3,093, including 84 and 4), or a lithographer and copper and steel plate printer (696, including 36 and 11), or a bookbinder (621, including 21 and 4). The slippers and the waistcoat are in red and the trousers in a refined muted green. Harold is thinking deeply!

21. Glaswegians. An amazing Miller and Lang postcard posted in Crieff on 25 December 1903. Immediately christened 'Kelvinside capers', this is beautifully drawn and coloured. The lady, for want of a better word, is dressed in black, with red and white socks, and little red cape trimmed with white, and a red hat with black feathers. The man on the bicycle with plus fours and deerstalker has a red jacket and a red and white striped shirt. Any similarity to living persons is purely coincidental!

I "I'm fou, absolutely fou."

250

22. Glaswegians. To many temperance supporters looking at the massive alcoholism and drunkenness in Victorian and Edwardian Glasgow this might almost be 'Mr. Glasgow'. This would not really be altogether fair for this Miller and Lang card, posted on 6 July 1903, clearly represents someone at the lower end of the social scale, rather than the hard-working and well-paid skilled and semi-skilled worker in heavy industry who would be rather more truly representative. As well as being fou the gentleman is almost certainly skint by now, and may well be on his way in the near future to join the 2,053 men and 1,923 women in the Barnhill, City and Govan Combination Poorhouses, or the 8,763 men and 1,020 women in Glasgow and Govan Licensed Common Lodging Houses in 1901.

CAFE

WATCHMAKERS CHAS L. REIS & Cᵒ JEWELLERS **GOLDSMITHS. CHAˢ. L. REIS & Cᵒ SILVERSMITHS** BIRMINGHAM DUBLIN & BELFAST ESTᴰ 1877

209-215 ARGYLE Sᵗ – 2&4 JAMAICA Sᵗ GLASGOW.

23. One of the most economical methods of advertising and attracting trade and of sending messages to customers was by using postcards at the ½d post rate. Many shops and businesses had cards made for their correspondence, or to send in packages and boxes, or just to give away to casual visitors and collectors. The most interesting cards include a photograph of the shop front. It was a common feature to include shop assistants and other staff standing outside the shop, and this may be the case here as far as the four persons to the right are concerned. Note the café above. In Glasgow in 1901 424 males were working as goldsmiths, silversmiths, and jewellers (including 52 employers and 43 working on their own account) and 99 females (including 4 employers).

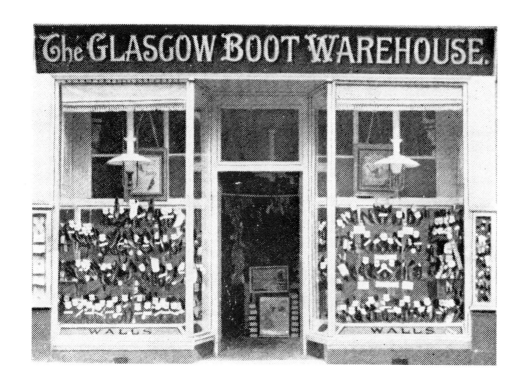

24. The Glasgow Boot Warehouse (about 1902-1907) is another good example of the advertising postcard. Note the extremely packed front areas – the general idea of window dressing seems to have been to have as many items as could possibly be crammed into the space. There were 315 males working as boot, shoe, patten, and clog dealers in Glasgow in 1901 (including 74 employers) and 606 females (14 employers). In addition there were 3,373 males working as boot and shoe-makers (248 employers) and 769 females (10 employers). This compares with 4,399 males listed as tailors (355 employers) and 130 males as shirtmakers and seamstresses; and 4,745 females as tailors, 6,246 as shirtmakers and seamstresses and 7,867 as dressmakers.

John Bull _ "If you please gentlemen, may I sit down somewhere?"
Chorus of Foreigners _ "Yes,_ try the corner"

25. A good example of a postcard purchased in large numbers, stamped on the back 'Scott's *Zollverein* Boots are the Best Boots on Earth. 32 Jamaica Street', and hence used to attract customers. The card was published by C.W. Faulkner and Co., London, and is a neat example of contemporary British xenophobia in the view of 'foreigners' expressed here. Perhaps this was related to Great Britain's general unpopularity in Europe and isolation during the Boer War. The subject of the postcard at least relates to the product being advertised.

TUCK'S POST CARD

CARTE POSTALE   POSTKARTE

PROCESSED IN HOLLAND.

(FOR ADDRESS ONLY)

School Books

SUPPLIED AT

3d. in the 1/- discount.

GRANT EDUCATIONAL CO., Ltd.,

91 and 93 Union Street, GLASGOW.

By Appointment.

26. An even more economical stratagem was to purchase a number of view cards, in this case a pleasant view of the North Shore at Blackpool, a topographical card no doubt produced in tens of thousands by the famous firm of Raphael Tuck and Sons. This was then stamped on the back, possibly in this case to slip into books purchased at the shop. Pre-1914 almost certainly given the notice at the top right corner where the ½d stamp was placed indicating that the card was processed in Holland. Note the current price, an astonishing £3.

27. An example of a postcard still in use in the late 1930s, although the photograph on the front is very much earlier. Stamped on the reverse for use by company representatives. 'Telegraphic address 'Takapeg' Glasgow. Telephone Central 1631 (Private Branch Exchange). 64 Waterloo Street, Glasgow, C.2. Our... intends waiting upon you on or about... John Begg Ltd.'

28. On one side the Glasgow of the opulent offices, banks and warehouses, and on the other the hundreds of small shops in the streets of the city and the suburbs. The 1901 Census lists 4,318 males (including 616 employers) as grocers, and tea, coffee and chocolate dealers, and 776 females (54 employers): in Govan 482 males (67 employers) and 95 females (9 employers): and in Partick 373 males (72) and 102 females (6). This tiny Cooper and Co. card, reproduction actual size, although the back is divided for 'Correspondence' and 'Address Only', was probably not used through the postal services but rather as a novelty item to hand out to customers. The display includes a notice addressed to 'Grandparents'.

29. A postcard issued by MacSymon's Stores Ltd.,
again reproduced actual size. Note the window
display, probably mostly earthenware, and the
tenements and shops on the other side of the
street accidentally reproduced by reflection on to the glass
at the top. Glasgow itself in 1901 still was a centre for
making china and coarser wares. The 1901 Census lists
954 males (14 employers) and 696 females (1
employer) as engaged in earthenware, china and
porcelain manufacture; and 192 males (64 employers)
and 414 females (5 employers) as brick, cement,
pottery and glass dealers. MacSymon's Stores might
have been included in the category of General Shop-
keepers and Dealers (undefined) with 563 males (39
employers) and 1,504 females (30 employers).

30 Truly a talking picture, from which it is almost possible to 'hear' the voices in the Glasgow patois. Interesting comments on housing problems in modestly affluent 'lower middle class' tenements. Note the furniture and extras in the room in the tenement house on the right, and the patterned carpet in the other house on the left, and in both houses the womens' dresses and the mens' decorated waistcoats and suits. A lively Art Publishing Company card posted in Greenock in 1905. The written message is good — 'Enjoying holiday... Went a sail on Monday. Started from Ayr. Nellie put off the boat at Troon sea sick. So stormy all tied to the boat with a rope to keep us on our feet.'

SHE RUBS MA WHISKERS CLEAN AFF WI' HER CHEEKS.

31. Novelty cards included an extraordinary variety of silks, and others with attachments of mirrors, wood, coin, tinsel, dried flowers, miniature calendars, real hair, fur, even small gramophone records. This is a more ordinary postcard, posted in 1907, by the Art Publishing Company of Glasgow and with a dazzlingly novel hall of mirrors effect. The period Scotch gallantry is very typical. The costume and dress are an hilarious mixture, the wife with a red and white striped skirt and white apron, and the man with an orange and red kilt, white sporran, red waistcoat, purple jacket, and green beret with red and black band, and quite weird shoes.

Glasgow Cathedral.

RELIABLE SERIES

32. A favourite ploy with postcard publishers was to print faked night views of public buildings, churches, ships, and trains. Sometimes the resulting panorama was deceptive as a moonlight silhouette made a mundane piece of architecture appear exciting and romantic and even distinguished. This does not apply to this card of the Cathedral which is here, as always, superb when viewed from the south-east. This postcard was by William Ritchie and Sons of Edinburgh in their Reliable Series.

"There was a sound of revelry by night"
Byron

33. The cat and the cathedral, or cacophony by night. A very human and endearing Miller and Lang National Series card posted in 1904 and set in Old Glasgow looking across to the Cathedral in the distance. Good house roof details and costume. Byron was almost as popular as Burns in nineteenth century Scotland, but it is a pity that the quotation had not come from Wee Willie Winkie by the Glasgow poet William Miller (1810-1872). The animals in his poem are less distraught however, as 'the cat's singin' grey thrums to the sleepin' hen/ the dog's speldert on the floor and disna gie a cheep', and it is, of course, Willie who is the centre of commotion and disturbance.

Glasgow   Corner of Duke Street and High Street

34. There are many examples of classical photographs being used in postcards. Nos. 34-40, part of a set of cards of exceptional interest on a British and European scale, were published in the Caledonia Series by J.A. McCulloch about 1903-04. These were taken from the photographic records commissioned by the City of Glasgow Improvement Trust and taken by Thomas Annan in 1868. The photographs, together with some others taken about 1877, were published by the Trust in 1878 or 1879. Two other editions, one published by James Maclehose and Sons and the other by T. and R. Annan and Sons, were published in 1900 with twelve later plates included. The postcards, which were printed in Germany, provided good quality, inexpensive and widely available copies of these magnificent sources on housing conditions in 'Old Glasgow' before the massive clearances by the Trust and the railway companies between 1866 and 1901. This almost aerial view of the heartland area of the High Street and Duke Street is perhaps the best starting point for examining these cards.

Glasgow   Old High St. looking South

35. The once elegant and prosperous High Street, Saltmarket and Gallowgate and the streets and the wilderness of closes off them constituted by the middle and third quarter of the nineteenth century one of the worst urban slums and high population density areas in Great Britain. Note in this view of the High Street looking south to the Tolbooth Steeple the cobbled street and stone pavement, streets barrows and carts, gas lighting, three and four storey tenements, crow-stepped gables, and the pawnbrokers with the sign of the three balls and the poultry shop next to it on the left. Useful for local historians both for the incidental information difficult to come across elsewhere and in providing a series of impressions of atmosphere and period.

Glasgow   Old Vennell off High Street

36. The McCulloch postcard was printed the wrong way round – the lettering on the board should read '...Tal Store' and on the fragment of a poster on the wall to the right below 'Lecture'. Note that the vennell is cobbled, possibly poor drainage, the mixture of two and four storey houses, the lines of hanging blankets or sheets at chimney level, the absence of gas lighting, and the adults and children at the doorways. The Annan views are especially good just because they were taken with the limited and practical aim of recording buildings and streets and are therefore less likely to have been distorted by any radical bias (no 'rent a mob' crowd of street urchins here) or a taste for the bizarre or picturesque. In spite of the gloom and the grime this is not in the modern 'groaning in the streets' tradition of documentary reporting. It might be unwise to assume that 'working class' life elsewhere in Glasgow at this time was necessarily as unpleasant: this is a record of a limited area and should be seen as such.

Glasgow   High St.

37. Postmarked 9 March 1904 and sent from Glasgow to Greenock. The written message (back and front) is entirely family gossip on Belle's mother's health, how Nellie's baby is improving every day, that Jeanie is to visit soon, and that mother wearies to hear what they are all about... all oblivious to the picture of the High Street about 1868 on the front. Good details of seventeenth and eighteenth century buildings, ground floor shops and arcade. The notices on the building on the left are for money lending, musical instruments, all kinds of mechanics: the upper floors of the two central houses, H. McIlvenny's Lodgings and Lodgings Working Mens and Travellers, are possibly empty; on the right the Glasgow Abstainers Mission Room with Sabbath Worship, Mothers Meeting Monday, Youth Meeting Tuesday, Temperance Meeting Friday, and Penny Savings Bank open on Saturday.

Glasgow   Prince's St. from King St.

38. King Street lies off the Trongate, a very congested area and by repute one of the worst for the 'wilder tribes' of Glasgow. Note the numbers 31 and 33 on the corner buildings left and right respectively. The postcard has been 'improved', perhaps in Germany, with the addition of a neat but rather too detailed and precise little sketch of the three men in the centre front (not in the Annan photograph). The barrel and the carts are in the original photograph, but a few minute figures may have been added at the far end of the street in the card. The building on the right is lettered Tron Parish School & Bell's School. The poster in the window underneath is advertising 'Teas 2/8'.

39. One of the classical Victorian photographs, taken in 1868 and showing the Main Street in Gorbals looking north. The ghostly 'moving people' of early photographs make a fascinating composition and the costume detail is very good under the difficult circumstances, especially the lady to the right of the doorway to the vaults on the right and the small child in the cart on the left just behind the 'Milk and Cream' sign. Note the lettering on the fine building (good quality stonework in the chimney) on the right – 'The Old Gorbals Wine, Spirit, and Malt Liquor Vaults... Established 1822', and the VR poster advertising the Militia under the 'Rutherglen Loan' sign to the right of the doorway.

Glasgow   Elphinstone Tower, Main St., Gorbals

40. The loving detail of this photograph perhaps reflects Thomas Annan's own personal interest in architecture rather than just the commission on which he was engaged here. And he also provided the photographs for 'The Old Country Houses of the Glasgow Gentry' and 'The Painted Windows of Glasgow Cathedral'. The tower house, next to the Vaults in 39, had been a fine building, with good stonework and an interesting roof line and corner turrets. The well-stocked Gorbals Hosiery and Shirt Warehouse below (89 Main Street) is owned by an R. Lambie. Note the ghostly figure in the doorway of a small woman or a girl in a shawl. The Vaults are advertising 'Intermediate Ale' at 4d per Imperial Quart and India Pale Ale, and have a number of posters possibly for theatre shows, including one for the 'Waverley' above the two little girls (whose heads have been touched up for the postcard).

41. The University of Glasgow commissioned Thomas Annan
to take photographs of the Old College buildings before the
move to Gilmorehill in 1870. These were also used as subjects
for postcards published by J.A. McCulloch in the Caledonia
Series and printed in Germany. The main entrance here was
the work of John Mylne and is certainly a most handsome
composition. Note the clock on the tower behind,
presumably recording the time, 3.25 in the afternoon, when
the photograph was taken. The children on the right are in a
variety of costume suggesting a range from affluence to, if
not poverty, at least a humbler status in society. The gentlemen on the left seem to be conspicuously well-fed!

Glasgow   Old College from College St.

42. Thomas Annan died in 1887. It is just possible that he took this photograph of the Saltmarket from London Street in 1885, but it seems more probable that it was taken by another member of the firm of T. and R. Annan and Sons founded in 1873. Note the tram lines: and from the left the Boot and Shoe Factory, Glasgow Cross Pawnbroking Office with the premises below including a sale room, bootmakers, W. Cochrane (not open), and a clothiers: and on the right the Funeral Office and the Stamping for Embroidery sign. The buildings are, on the whole, well maintained and the general atmosphere quite different from that in the 1868 views.

43. The T. and R. Annan photograph of Bridgegate from the corner of Market Street taken in 1899. Very much in the style of the 1868 photographs, but the buildings are again in good order and the people are much better dressed. Their air of confidence, of course, may also be a matter of being accustomed to street photography. The panoply of advertisements is wonderful from Gallaher's Hammer Head Sixpenny Plug, Smith's Thick Black Roll Tobacco, Dick's Patent Belting, Swan Soap, Ardrossan and Belfast Steamers, Kirker Greer Old Irish Whisky, Lifebuoy Soap and White's Baby Carriages to Remylina Cornflour. Note McDougall and Sons Glass and China Show Rooms in the second building on the right.

Thatched Houses, Ladywell Street, Glasgow.

44. Postcards 44–51 were published in the Reliable Series by William Ritchie and Sons of Edinburgh in the 1900s. It is tempting to attribute these photographs to T. and R. Annan and Sons, and certainly some are very much in what might be termed the traditional Annan style. Dating is not easy, but in most cases is probably to the late 1880s or 1890s. Ladywell Street runs from south of the Necropolis to Duke Street. The houses, roofing, including thatching, windows and forestairs appear to be well maintained. Note the tramlines in the foreground; the Lorne Dairy ('141' on the wall under 'Lorne') and 'Ladywell Street' under 'Dairy'; and the woman in the shawl in the foreground carrying a very well-dressed child in a smart coat and cap.

The Saracen's Head Inn, Gallowgate, Glasgow, Whence the Mail Coaches started for London.

45. Posted on 6 July 1908 from Glasgow to Notting Hill in London. Unusually this appears to be a winter scene with snow at the edge of the road and on the pavement on the left and lying up against the walls of the buildings. Perhaps April snowshowers mixed with sunshine, as one shop has sunblinds down! Very clear tramlines. Ground floor shops include A.J. Cruden (drapers?), Kane and Co. (not open), a hairdresser and a shop selling ice cream.

Washing Day. Entrance to Court, Saracen's Head Inn, Gallowgate, Glasgow, RELIABLE [WB] SERIE

46. Possibly a photograph taken at the same time as 45; otherwise almost impossible to date, as this could almost as easily be the 1860s as the 1890s. Comic or ethnic cards showing a 'Scotch Washing' in various guises are commonplace, but straightforward and simply realistic washing tub photographs are scarce. Indeed evidence of ordinary everyday activities is hard to find, and photographs of house interiors in poorer areas virtually non-existent until much later. A good picture of the hard physical labour involved. The little boy at the left is looking at the photographer as if puzzled by his interest in the washerwomen. The huge wooden shutters are interesting – perhaps a suggestion here of the former importance of the inn.

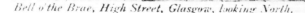

Bell o'the Brae, High Street, Glasgow, looking North.

RELIABLE SERIES

47. The Bell O' the Brae was at the steepest and highest part of the High Street. Note the Globe Loan Office and R. and J. Templeton below on the left; and the Oil and Colour Store, selling paraffin and oil lamps in the corner building on the right. The woman resting against the cart in the left foreground appears to be knitting. Perhaps an earlier photograph if the absence of tram lines is relevant evidence here.

Mumford's Theatre, Foot of Saltmarket, Glasgow.

RELIABLE WE SERIES

48. Tramlines and the gentleman in tweedy looking suit and cap suggest a later date for this view of the Saltmarket. The main business, John Cornin's Wholesale and Retail New and Secondhand Clothing, offers 'The Highest Price Given For Ladies and Gentlemens Cast off Clothing'. E. Caldwell on the left at 177 is also a new and secondhand clothing dealer.

49. Looking up the corner of Saltmarket and Bridgegate to
the railway line behind. Tramlines difficult to make out in
this picture. Tenement on the right in the modern style of
the late nineteenth century. The premises below are offering
fish dinners and fish teas. Quite a little group of young men
about town at the corner. The young woman moving in their
direction with a purposeful air is wearing a tartan shawl. Note
the Undertaking Company on the left advertising that 'Every
Requisite For Interments May Be Had Here'. The shop below
appears to be mainly men's secondhand clothing.

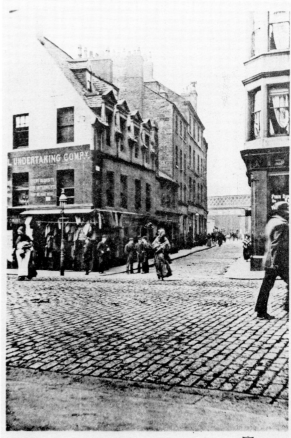

*Old Ship Bank, Corner of Saltmarket
and Bridgegate, Glasgow.*

RELIABLE SERIES.

Bridgegate, Glasgow, looking to Saltmarket.

50. Probably an earlier view of the Bridgegate than 43, taken from almost the same place. Almost an individual portrait of the man in the centre showing his face in considerable detail. The young woman at the cart looking straight towards the photographer seems to welcome the prospect of immortality attained through the lens of a camera; the three on the right seem to disapprove, and the girl on her left is attempting a wry smile. Of course, this is reading far too much into facial expressions, but the photograph is sufficiently clear for this to possible, however unwise.

Nelson Street, Glasgow (off Trongate).

51. A very carefully posed, calm photograph with an enormous amount of detail. On the right Rawson and Anderson of Strabane, Ireland, are offering a great sale of their entire stock amounting to £1,232 16/9. Other firms include Quigleys on the right and Grainger, Templeman and Smith on the left. The crate or basket in the centre is a superb idea, probably just coincidence no doubt, but perfect for this street, and the workman in shirt and waistcoat with his dog and a small boy walking along behind make up a beautifully balanced composition. Note the rather fine ground floor shops with painted frontages. The street has the peace and calm hoped for in pedestrian precincts to-day.

Glasgow Cathedral.

RELIABLE SERIES.

Thanks for P.P.C. How is this for your collection. J.I.

52. An undivided back sent to a collector near Cumbernauld Station on 14 October 1902. The view of the Cathedral from the south-east shows the hill on which it sits and the impressive east end. To the west are Robert Adam's Royal Infirmary of 1792-93 (demolished in 1907) with its handsome dome, and the rather Gothic Barony Free Church spire of 1866-67. Glasgow may seem from some photographs to be dominated by church spires; but the numbers of clergy were less than these suggest. The 1901 Census for Glasgow lists 125 Church of Scotland and 206 United Free Church ministers, 29 Episcopalian clerics, 83 Roman Catholic priests, 5 monks, 103 ministers and priests in other religious groups, 125 male and 107 female missionaries, scripture readers and itinerant preachers, and 14 nuns and Sisters of Charity.

Glasgow Cathedral

53. A London and North Western Railway Company card published between 1904 and 1906 and posted on 16 February 1906 to a collector in Holland. Official postcards showing the crest or name of one of the many railway companies were purchased in huge numbers at railway stations (over 11 million LNWR cards were sold between 1904 and 1914). The Necropolis to the right of the Cathedral, which is seen here from the south-west, was laid out between 1831 and 1833. It is one of the most splendid 'cities of the dead' in Britain, with work by many of the distinguished architects employed in Glasgow, including David Hamilton, John Bryce and John Baird. Note also the tenement blocks to the north of the Cathedral.

The People's Palace, Glasgow.

Our house just faces this beautiful piece of Architecture.

RELIABLE SERIES.

54. Another Reliable Series card posted in Glasgow on 15 April 1904 – 'Hoping this will prove to be a masterpiece to add to your collection' – by Algy, who mentions that his house 'faces this beautiful piece of architecture'. The People's Palace was opened in 1898, not so much essentially as a museum but rather as a cultural centre and institute for the East End of Glasgow: and like its namesake in East London a 'palace for the people' to be 'open, free and forever'. It was to be an art gallery and a museum, a winter garden and a place for concerts and variety entertainments.

55. The old centre of Glasgow, the Trongate, about 1899-1900. The horse-drawn trams (replaced by electric trams in 1901) are particularly interesting. Businesses include the Tron Steeple Boot Depot, and to the right Percy Bros. and then Stewarts (advertising Stewart's Waxworks). The Tron Steeple was added to what had formerly been the collegiate church of S. Mary and S. Ann post 1592: the spire was added between 1630 and 1636. The church was destroyed by fire in the late eighteenth century and rebuilt in 1793-94 to the south of and detatched from the Steeple. The arches over the pavement were inserted in 1855.

The Cross & Trongate, Glasgow.

RELIABLE [WH] SERIES.

56. A Reliable Series postcard showing the Trongate and the Tron Steeple from the east. Note the electric trams and the tram wires. The tram on the left is going to Ibrox. The Glasgow tramway system was a major employer and the 1901 Census lists 1,539 men and boys as working for the Tramway Service, plus 86 living in Govan and 171 in Partick, and 5 women in Glasgow. In spite of this development from horse-drawn to electric trams local transport in Glasgow, as elsewhere in Britain, was still in the 1900s essentially a horse economy with thousands of working horses pulling carts, vans, and waggons singly, in pairs and in teams. The millions of tons of merchandise carried annually by the railways were still collected and distributed locally by horse-hauled vehicles. Note the carts here on the left and in front of the tram on the right; and also the congested pavements with an odd ratio of about thirty men to one woman.

57. An Annan photograph about 1902 of Crown Street in the Gorbals looking north across the Albert Bridge to William Stark's Justiciary Court House (1807-1814) on the left. Note the open deck tram in the centre, with a full top load, and the tram lines and wires. A delightful vignette in the foreground of a little boy with bare feet resting on the tram line and a prosperous looking businessman bearing down on him; two women in shawls on the left, but on the whole well-dressed men, women and children giving an impression of a successful free economy. Nearly all the housing in Edwardian Glasgow was privately owned, and rented, and at the outbreak of the Great War Glasgow Corporation owned merely about 1.4% of the housing stock. The shop at the corner of Govan Street on the right is McLean Wine Merchant.

Glasgow Bridge

Glasgow

58. Glasgow (or Jamaica or Broomielaw) Bridge in a Caledonia Series card posted 18 February 1905. The Caledonian Railway Central Station Bridge is on the left and Custom House Quay and Clyde Street are on the right. Glasgow Bridge was completed between 1894 and 1899 replacing and using the façade of the earlier Thomas Telford bridge. A typical scene with many carts, open deck trams, gigs and pedestrians. Note OXO prominently advertised on the sheds on the Quay, and Paisley's Tailoring Establishment Foreign and Colonial Outfitter between the railway and road bridges; and St. Enoch Church spire and St. Enoch Station Hotel on the right behind the Quay.

59. Glasgow Bridge and Central Station on a card posted 18 August 1913. Closed top trams with an action sequence on the left as two men (possibly tramway staff?) jump on to the moving tramcar. The impressive scale of the railway structures may suggest the importance of Glasgow as the centre of a railway network. In the 1901 Census railway employees living in Glasgow included 1,662 officials and clerks, 1,327 engine drivers and stokers, 755 guards, 382 signalmen, 221 patrolmen and level crossing men, 418 platelayers, gangers and packers, 678 labourers, 2,402 porters and servants, and 29 female officials and clerks and 27 female porters and servants. There were another 312 men in Govan and 280 men in Partick employed on the railway.

60. St. Enoch Square on a Wrench Series card posted in Glasgow on 18 August 1908 to a lady living in Jersey. The centrepiece is the curious out-of-scale headquarters building of the Glasgow Subway (underground railway) built in 1895-96 to plans by James Miller. It does seem very odd in comparison to the massive buildings round about it, in particular the St. Enoch Station and St. Enoch Hotel block built between 1870 and 1879. The City of Glasgow Union Railway was taken over by the Glasgow and South Western Railway. Note the impressive cast iron structures in the foreground in front of the Subway offices and station.

Argyle Street, Glasgow   *When are you coming to shop here?*

61. The classic view of Argyle Street posted in Glasgow on 14 December 1903 as a birthday card to a lady in Canterbury. Immensely congested, and suggesting some of the traffic problems of the period – a traffic 'jam' is not a phenomenon confined to the motor car era. Note the single deck tram on the left going to London Road and the open top double deck tram on the right. A summer day photograph judging by all the sun shades – the one in the left foreground is carrying lettering advertising Howell's Tobacco. The building above is a hotel. The store on the right with huge numbers on the pavement outside is Robert Simpson's, subsequently Arnott Simpsons.

62. A postcard cluttered up with tartan, what looks like heather, and heraldic work of doubtful relevance to the subject. But otherwise a well-defined photograph about 1910 of Renfield Street with St. Vincent Street in the right and left foreground, and looking north to West George Street (visible on the left). This is very much the prosperous Edwardian Glasgow of offices, banks, city businessmen, well-dressed couples and fashionable ladies visiting their legal and financial advisers and/or the elegant little shops in the area.

63. Buchanan Street was the best street in Edwardian Glasgow, the best architecturally, with the best shops, the most important banks, and fine opulent offices and clubs. Moreover it was kept clear of trams which made an enormous difference to the general tone and calm atmosphere compared to Argyle Street or Sauchiehall Street, and of course was easily accessible from the railway stations and the main tram routes. The offices being completed here, a large red sandstone building at the corner of Springfield Court with voluptuous statuary at the front, were completed in 1898, so this photograph was probably taken around 1897. Note the variety of horse-drawn transport, including the 'bus' with the Nestle's Milk advertisement and a uniformed conductor, and the street furniture (lamp standards and post boxes included).

Buchanan Street, Glasgow.

RELIABLE WR SS SERIES.

64. A Reliable Series card posted 9 September 1903, with a view of Buchanan Street from almost the same angle as in 63. Compare the roof details of the now complete building in the right centre with its position while still under construction. Note Argyle Chambers and the Argyle Arcade on the right; and the immense variety of gigs, carriages, cabs, carts and waggons and the differences in the clothes and indeed uniforms worn by the drivers. To keep these equipped was an industry in itself. Glasgow in 1901, for example, had 530 men and boys listed as saddlers and harness and whip makers, including 39 employers, and 34 women and girls likewise engaged.

65. A coloured card posted 2 August 1908 showing the Argyle Arcade, which runs from Buchanan Street to Argyle Street. The cast-iron hammer-beam roof was designed by John Baird in 1827. Baird also designed the famous Gardner's Building in Jamaica Street in 1855-56. The Arcade seems to blend in so perfectly with the Edwardian period. Note the excessively fussy and crammed window displays, and the electric lighting suspended from the roof (and an older lighting system).

Buchanan Street, Glasgow.

66. A postcard published by F. Bauermeister and printed in Germany about 1905. An exquisite photograph with very good details, including 'Nelson, Shaw and Macgregor Silk Mercers, Linen and Woollen Drapers' on the first shop on the right, 'The American Shoe Company' at 59 which is the first shop on the left, and the closed waggon, second left, which is a 'Caledonian Railway Parcel Van'. It does look almost idyllically peaceful, but from at least one point of view this is deceptive as, in fact, runaway horses and street accidents were commonplace as almost anything out of the usual could frighten a horse and make it bolt. Broken limbs and worse were everyday happenings.

Buchanan Street, Glasgow

10/9/03 Gay wet the day & still moist, raining the noo:—

Uncle Mark

67. Un undivided back posted in Glasgow on September 10, 1903 and sent to a lady in Newcastle, Staffs. Taken from slightly further along the street than 66. Details include a boy on the left at the edge of the street carrying a billboard, one of Cranstons Tea Rooms on the right, at least one dandy with a light coloured waistcoat, and the loaded carts and the cabs and carriages. It may still be surprising to read that in Glasgow in 1901 10,747 men and boys were working as carmen, carriers, carters and waggoners and 2,133 as coachmen, grooms and cabmen. There were also 11 women and girls as carmen, carriers, carters and waggoners.

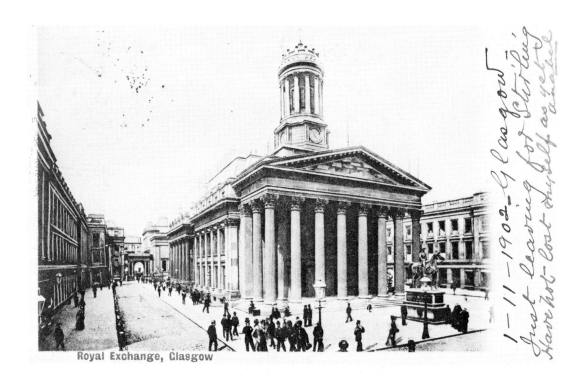

Royal Exchange, Glasgow

68. An undivided back posted in Glasgow on 1 November 1902 showing perhaps the best square in Glasgow. The centrepiece is the Royal Exchange by David Hamilton, built 1827-1832, which incorporates in the eastern half behind the Corinthian portico and underneath the cupola the Cunninghame Mansion of 1775-1778. Royal Exchange Place by David Hamilton and James Smith, built 1830-1839, is most impressive and elegant. Some of the figures in the foreground look as if they are sketches added at some stage to the photograph.

69. George Square was laid out as part of Glasgow's late eighteenth century 'new town'. The buildings on the left at the north-east corner of the Square and built 1807-1818 perhaps suggest something of the excellent proportions and charm of the original whole, which was probably enhanced by the 80 feet high Doric column with the statue of Scott erected in 1838. By the late nineteenth century, however, with the movement of the General Post Office from Bridgegate and the erection of the City Chambers between 1883 and 1888, George Square had become the 'centre' of the city. The City Chambers are a perfect and enduring expression ot the pride, wealth, power and taste for opulence of an era of triumphant capitalism and speculative free enterprise. Note the cab shelter on the north side of the Square, the horse-drawn trams and the iron railings. Photograph about 1900.

70. The full frontal view of the City Chambers with electric trams and tram wires around 1905. In spite of the success and the scale of the Corporation's investment in and management of the tramway system, Glasgow was a free enterprise city in the 1900s. In the 1900 General Election in Glasgow, Govan and Partick four Conservatives were elected (Blackfriars and Hutchesontown, Bridgeton, Central – unopposed, and College), four Liberal Unionists (Camlachie, St. Rollox, Tradeston and Partick), and one Liberal (Govan). Conservative candidates received 21,371 votes, Liberal Unionists 21,946, Liberals 28,851 and a joint Liberal/Labour candidate 2,785.

Sauchiehall Street, Glasgow.

RELIABLE SERIES.

71. An undivided back card in the Reliable Series posted in Glasgow on 15 December 1902 as local mail to a lady in Hillhead. Is the written message in code, or is it some form of dialect? At any rate Lizzie's language is obscure. The open deck electric tram is bound for Anniesland. A shop on the left is advertising 'New Etchings by D Y Cameron'. The first shop on the right is 'P & P Campbell Dyer and Cleaners', advertising 'Perth Dye'; next to this there is a 'Bookseller', just to the right of the horse and cart loaded with timber; and 'Donald E Cameron, L.D.S., Dentist' has rooms above. Note the very impressive electric lighting along Sauchiehall Street.

72. This later undated card shows Sauchiehall Street as part of a townscape dominated by tram wires and tram lines. Simpson's Music Sellers at the corner on the left has its windows full of illustrated sheet music and carries advertising for 'Scotch Songs', 'Irish Songs', 'Lists Free'; and behind note the electrically lighted sign for Boots, the Cash Chemists, at 101 Sauchiehall Street. Note on the right Lumley's Athletic (Rooms) with 'Billiard and Bagatelle Tables', 'Summer Sports' and 'Winter Pastimes'; and underneath at 76 Sauchiehall Street Lauder's public house on a valuable corner site convenient for theatreland. Glasgow's Census of Occupations in 1901 listed 1,996 barmen (plus 129 women); 1,128 inn and hotel keepers, publicans, and wine and spirit merchants (plus 128 women); 273 cellarmen (plus 41 women); and 1,243 others in inn, hotel and eating house service (plus 1,340 women).

Charing Cross, Glasgow.

73. This early and unused card carries no information about the publisher. It is a happy thought that it might have been F. Bauermeister, the foreign bookseller and publisher, whose house address post about 1908 was at 5 Charing Cross Mansions and from 1910 at 20 Charing Cross Mansions. The Mansions, designed by J.J. Burnet and completed in 1891, is an elaborate red sandstone 'waltz in stone'. In this card it is at the centre background with shops below and the impressive circular tower above. Note the line of carts on the left and the open deck tram (905) which is going to Kelvingrove.

Charing Cross and Grand Hotel.

Glasgow.

I hope you & Father are enjoying your ...

74. This Hartmann card posted in Glasgow in 1903 shows the rather splendid Grand Hotel in some detail and the Charing Cross Branch Post Office below. Charing Cross and Sauchiehall Street to the east had some very good firms selling and making furniture, including Reynolds and McCulloch at Charing Cross. The importance of this service industry can be gauged from the numbers employed in Glasgow in 1901, including 2,438 cabinet makers (plus 13 women); 306 French polishers (plus 1,202 women); 930 upholsterers (499); 671 wood carvers and gilders (93); 145 willow, cane and rush workers and basket makers (19); and 340 furniture dealers (131).

Kelvin Bridge & Great Western Road. *Glasgow.*

75. This Hartmann card in delicate faded tinting, posted in Glasgow on 8 October 1904, shows Kelvin Bridge, opened in 1891, and the tenements and churches to the east on Great Western Road. Landsdowne United Presbyterian Church (with the tall spire) by John Honeyman 1862-63 is one of the most pleasing Victorian churches in Glasgow with a lightness and grace usually lacking in such buildings. The second spire belongs to St. Mary's Episcopal Cathedral, surprisingly by George Gilbert Scott 1870-1874 with the spire added in 1893. Note the decorative triplet lamps on the bridge.

Kelvinbridge, Great Western Road, Glasgow.

76. This Caledonia Series card was printed in Germany and is particularly delicately tinted in pinks and creams with yellow lettering and bands for the Glasgow Corporation tramcar and pink, blue and green stripes on the shop sun shades on the left. A great deal of new building was taking place to the west of here in the 1890s and 1900s and Glasgow in 1901 had a very large (male) work force engaged on building and other construction activities. These included, with the number of females in brackets, 411 builders (1) and 55 builders' labourers, 6,685 carpenters and joiners (1), 1,438 bricklayers and 746 bricklayers' labourers, 3,164 masons (16) and 1,829 masons' labourers, 1,637 slaters and tilers (4), 1,047 plasterers and 384 plasterers's labourers, 19 paperhangers and whitewashers, 4,047 painters, decorators and glaziers (32), 2,469 plumbers (5), 231 gasfitters and 32 locksmiths and bellhangers.

Kibble Palace in Botanic Gardens — Glasgow

1952

77. This Hartmann card was posted in Glasgow in 1903 to a collector in Stonehaven to wish him 'a ripping time at Southport'! Every possible space is used for writing including the bit where the writer gets his lines in upside down below the picture. Mr. Kibble of Coulport on Loch Long initially offered the spectacular Kibble Crystal Art Palace and Conservatory to Queen's Park, who declined to accept it and so instead it ended up at the Botanic Gardens. It was taken down at Coulport in 1872 and erected at the Gardens in 1873. The larger of the two domes, 40 feet high and 150 feet diameter, was thought at that time to have space for between 6,000 and 8,000 people.

78. This Caledonia Series card was posted in Glasgow on 4 October 1905 to a lady in Sussex with the message that the writer hopes 'to be in Aberdeen to-morrow'. The typically frayed corner is actually the layer, with the delicately tinted scene of Great Western Road at Botanic Gardens, coming apart from the thicker textured back of the card. The open deck tram on the left is going to Kelvinside. Note the richly decorated street furniture of pavements and islands, and James Miller's Botanic Gardens Station of about 1894, with the domed minaret-like towers, built for the Glasgow Central Railway and opened about 1896.

Byres Road, Partick

Valentines Series

79. This Valentine Series card was posted in Glasgow on 16 September 1904 to friends or relations in Gairloch in Ross-shire. The open deck tram (555) on the left is going up Byres Road to Botanic Gardens, but essentially this is a 'horse economy' card with the cart and gigs and cabs behind. The shops on the left include a general merchants, with a Frys Chocolate advertisement in the window display, and a dairy. Note the contrast in styles between the rather superior tenements on the left and the plainer less prestigious buildings on the right.

The "Soft" Lodger
Going for Messages.

THE
"SOFT" LODGER SERIES.

80. The 'Soft Lodger' series with the lively and gentle humour characteristic of the Miller and Lang National Series was very popular, since it did reflect some of the everyday experiences and problems of thousands of business people, workmen and students in Glasgow and in other cities and towns in Edwardian Britain. The dominant landlady was obviously a popular bogey figure. The dress and costume of children, lodger and landlady alike suggest an area such as Hillhead, Langside or Pollokshields.

81. This Miller and Lang card was posted in Leslie on 2 November 1906. Note again the fairly prosperous, but rather 'common' lodger − compare the check jacket and bowtie in 80 and the waistcoat and checked trousers here − settling down to a rather spartan supper of thick wholesome biscuit, butter and pickled sausage from Chicago. The American connection is interesting, because Chicago was the nearest equivalent in the United States to Glasgow as a bustling centre of commerce and industry, and because there were innumerable connections between emigrant Scots in North America and their families and friends in Glasgow and the West of Scotland. What the lodger thinks he has again is an alcohol derived condition which the vast numbers of temperance supporters of the period would have immediately recognised.

Glasgow University

Where our "Rising Sun" is to shine

82. The best view of George Gilbert Scott's University of Glasgow 1866-1872 (and the tower by J. Oldrid Scott added in 1887) is presented is this card posted on 12 October 1903 to a lady in Canterbury. 'Mrs D. has grown so stout. Hollidge is still hovering around... The card collecting mania is still strong here.' The building had 5 miles of hot-water pipes: and 2,000,000 cubic feet of fresh air drawn from the tower could be propelled through it every hour using the suction power of heated flues. Students were consigned in the 1901 Census to the last occupational category of XXIII, that is 'Without Specified Occupation or Unoccupied. Others aged 10 years and upwards (including students)'. In Glasgow these were 33,140 males and 185,003 females.

83. T. and R. Annan and Sons took a series of photographs in 1905 from the University tower. The remarkable view to the south-west looking along the line of the River Kelvin includes Partick Bridge built 1877-78 for the Glasgow and Yoker Turnpike Trust in the centre, and Partick Sewage Pumping Station, just completed in 1904, on the right; further south on the left the Regent Flour Mills built 1887-1890 with a six storey warehouse on Bunhouse Road and the mill at the riverside; and on the right the Scotstoun Flour Mills of 1877 with the five storey building on the riverside built in 1898. Note the open space, later the site of Kelvin Hall, and the building operations underway in the right foreground (part of the Western Infirmary).

84. This photograph shows Partick Bridge with a coal wart, carrying an advertisement for 'Best House Coal', and another cart and waggon moving at a leisurely pace east towards the Kelvingrove Art Gallery, about 1905. The Art Gallery was completed in 1901 to be used in the International Exhibition of that year and then opened in 1902 as a gallery. Coal was still 'King' in Glasgow in 1901. There were still 2,013 coal and shale miners living in Glasgow itself, 34 mine owners, agents and managers, and 811 coal and coke merchants and dealers (including 241 employers). For Govan and Partick respectively add 23,1 and 75 and 17,3 and 80.

Springburn Road   Glasgow

85. This Caledonia Series card was posted in Glasgow on 23 October 1904 to a gentleman in Hoddam near Ecclefechan. 'D.V. I will be with you on Monday leaving with the 10 a.m. ... for the Event.' At first glance the tenement street in Springburn seems to be made up of lines of unvarying monotony, but a closer inspection shows a considerable amount of decorative detail and variety in windows and pediments and cornices. The horse and cart have a load of rolls of carpets (or linoleum). Glasgow in 1901 had 563 males and 1,182 females working in carpet, rug and felt manufacture.

The Cottar's Saturday Night.

SALE PRICES

EGGS & BACON

SPECIAL

FOOTBALL EDITION

BEER

Moral:

Think not of to-morrow

86. This Art Publishing Company card was posted in Arbroath on 27 July 1905. 'I suppose you and your Grand Father have been out on your motors every day. I hope you havent burst your tyres.' The sketch is perhaps a patrician view from Hyndland of 'working class' Glasgow (Maryhill or Springburn, for example) on a Saturday night. Pa, ma and the weans look as if they are back from a trip doon th' watter, and having spent all their money are having to walk home rather than take a tram. If this is Maryhill then *he* is a Partick Thistle supporter, and has seen the Saturday football results in the Football Edition under his left arm; *she* is dressed in the very latest in bad taste. Butchers sold off their meat cheaply on a Saturday night, hence the 'Sale Prices' notice behind.

The Cross, Springburn

87. The highlight of this street scene at Springburn Cross is the superb poster art, including Will's Cigarettes and Whitbread's Stout. The shop on the right is a hatter. The tram (832) is going to Rouken Glen. The man to the right of the tram is pushing a cart with a (milk) churn. The children, some 20 or 21 in all, are an interesting mixture. At least eight of the boys are barefoot, but possibly only one girl. The girl on the left is carrying a baby. It is very difficult to estimate their ages, but most look to be 8 or 9 years old, with perhaps some a few years older. They must have been posed here by the Valentine photographer, so this does raise the question of whether they are really a typical group for the area or not. Are they selected at random, or because they are better or worse dressed than others?

Workers leaving Singer's Sewing Machine Works, Kilbowie

88. Postcards of streets and tenements help to bring to life statistics on overcrowding and population structure, but rather fewer give any idea of how the hard-working, skilled and disciplined work force in the West of Scotland spent their lives in an industrial context. This card, published by W.G. Leslie, 202 Church Street, Maryhill, and posted in Clydebank on 12 July 1907, shows one group of workers en masse, although not in Glasgow itself but at the Sewing Machine Works at Kilbowie. So clear is the detail that the 70 or 80 men at the front are virtually individual portraits. The steam train at the right and the passengers on the platform were sketched in as later additions. Note also the small steam engine and waggons in the centre left below the clock.

CANNIESBURN TOLL. GLASGOW   RELIABLE SERIES 4040/138

89. Glasgow was an overcrowded city with enormous numbers of children living in homes and closes and streets in many poorer 'working class' areas under the constant pressure of the sheer numbers of brothers, sisters, cousins, aunts, uncles and inquisitive neighbours. Privacy was the luxury of a few. Overcrowding in the home could just as well exist in a country cottage as in a tenement, but other circumstances were quite different. This Reliable Series card posted on 7 October 1910 from Great Western Road to go to Scotstoun shows Canniesburn Toll in the days of the 'horse economy'. Many later virtually or actually suburban areas were still largely rural in the 1900s.

The Pond in Whiteinch Park, Glasgow.

RELIABLE SERIES.

90. This Reliable Series card was posted in Glasgow on 17 July 1905 to a collector in Portsmouth. The view is of the Pond in Whiteinch Park, but it could be almost any park in any part of Great Britain for many photographers admirably captured one aspect of the atmosphere of the era in these studies of groups of three, four, or five little boys beside a burn or a river or a pond. To many who remember the Somme or Gallipoli in the Great War these photographs are almost unbearably sad, for how many of these boys were wasted, absolutely the operative word, 'For King and Country' fighting other little boys who likewise had collected postcards and been photographed for them at German boating ponds and streams? Few looking at this card in 1905 would have dreamt that such foolishness on such a scale was possible.

Lake. in Victoria Park, Whiteinch.

91. This card was posted in Scotstoun on 7 July 1907 to Collessie in Fife. It makes a charming period piece park scene with the well-dressed children in really quite voluptuous clothes engaged in a leisure pastime popular all over Edwardian Britain. In one respect it is fundamentally different from a photograph taken in the 1980s, and that is the notable absence of old people. The population of Glasgow in 1901 looks extraordinarily young with all those huge numbers of children – 122,553 boys and 122,581 girls (what admirable symmetry) under 15 years of age – and the few elderly citizens perhaps almost valued for their rarity, for there were only 17,148 men and 24,117 women aged 60 years and above.

Queen's Park Ponds, *Glasgow.*

92. This card, published by Chas. L. Reis, the Jewellers, of Glasgow, Dublin and Belfast (see 23) was posted on 24 May 1905. As so often with early photographs, of course, everyone appears to look rather solemn and purposeful and it is difficult to catch the light-hearted pleasure taken by the participants in the sailing and racing of their miniature ships and yachts. The Glasgow parks and gardens all appear to be beautifully kept, indeed immaculate, with the absence of litter a conspicuous point whether in the Botanic Gardens, Alexandra Park, Glasgow Green, Kelvingrove Park or Queen's Park as here. Glasgow from the 1901 Census had 503 men and boys working as gardeners, nurserymen, seedsmen and florists (and 22 women and girls) and 72 domestic gardeners. For Govan and Partick the totals are 64 and 3, and 104 and 15 respectively.

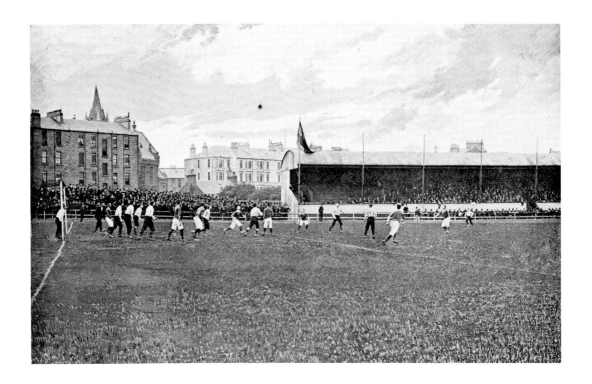

93. This early sporting photograph of Cathkin Braes or Cathkin Park Football Ground shows not a game involving Third Lanark F.C., but instead a match on 26 May 1895 between Celtic and Rangers Football Clubs. 'Spot the Ball' enthusiasts will note the expertise with which the photographer has added the football in the upper left centre area. The jerseys, knickerbockers and stockings look remarkably uncomfortable – and all for the sake of propriety! Rangers are in the traditional royal blue shirts and white knickerbockers, and Celtic in green and white striped shirts and green or black knickerbockers, the official attire between 1888 and 1904.

94. This Miller and Lang National Series card was posted on 21 May 1909 to Master Robt. Brown in Edinburgh. 'Hope you are a good boy *not* playing football. Tell Jeanie another of the black hens died yesterday.' The injunction almost certainly refers to street football, with the overtones of the propriety expected of 'good' boys from 'respectable' homes. Note the shorts rather than trousers or knickerbockers; but the boots seem flimsy, so perhaps this is not entirely satisfactory evidence of what footballers were wearing at the time. Glasgow was already a city of football fanatics, with Celtic (founded in 1867), Queens Park (1867), Third (Lanark (1872), Rangers (1872), Partick Thistle (1875) and Clyde (1877) all having support drawn from their own areas, but with Rangers and Celtic also unfortunately attracting elements more concerned with the religious and political affiliations of these clubs.

THE BAND STAND, ROUKEN GLEN.

95. This Miller and Lang National Series card is undated, but is probably from about 1910. Rouken Glen had been purchased from the Crums by Lord Rowallan and presented to Glasgow Corporation to become what was effectively a country park for the city. The three men in the foreground and the bicycles against the tree on the left suggest that this was a carefully arranged photograph. It combines the popular afternoon pastimes of listening to the (military) band, cycling and taking a walk in the park. Most of the visitors from Glasgow would have taken the trams, by then extended from Thornliebank and Giffnock to Rouken Glen, out from the city. Note that hardly anyone dares to go without a hat, cap or bonnet of some sort. In Glasgow in 1901 there were 412 women and 68 men occupied as makers of hats, caps and bonnets, 1,203 women and 8 men as milliners, and 112 women and 148 men were hat, bonnet, and straw plait dealers.

TEA ROOMS, ROUKEN GLEN.

96. This Record Series card published by Wm Nimmo and Co. of Edinburgh was posted in Glasgow on 9 June 1908. An afternoon walk for the more affluent traditionally included a stop at the 'Rouken Glen Tea Rooms'. Note the staff in the doorway and the well-dressed customers, all looking placidly, like a well-trained audience, at the photographer. Did the tearoom make their own bread and cakes? If not Glasgow had a considerable service industry doing just this, with in 1901 3,513 men and boys and 1,655 women and girls working as bakers and biscuit and cake makers, 1,004 and 1,655 working for bakers and confectioners (dealers), and 146 and 1,278 working for jam, preserve and sweet makers.

FEEDING THE SWANS, ROUKEN GLEN   19. 9. 15.

97. This W. Ritchie and Sons Twilight Series card, printed in Saxony, is dated 19-9-15 on the front, but it was almost certainly published before the outbreak of the Great War in 1914. The photograph, of course, could have just as easily been taken in the 1900s and in Edinburgh or London as in Glasgow. The dress is charming, the detail of the ducks and swans and bushes is excellent, and the oval setting is a popular Victorian and Edwardian format for a photograph frame. It was possible for the wives of the more prosperous and successful citizens of Glasgow to turn out their children in these fashionable clothes because of the assistance of the 'army' of 16,241 female domestic servants and because of the size of the laundry and washing service industry which employed 3,496 women and girls and 81 men and boys (totals for 1901).

THORNLIEBANK SCHOOL.

98. This decorative card, published by Kelso, Draper and Stationer, Thornliebank, was posted in Glasgow on 4 July 1910 to Co. Antrim in Ireland. The open deck tramcar is on the Giffnock and Rouken Glen route, a service which took Glaswegians out of the city well into Renfrewshire and into quite a rural environment at that date. By 1914 Glasgow Corporation Tramways had some 851 trams on 197 miles of track. Thornliebank was still essentially a nineteenth century village developed for the cotton printing industry: its inhabitants included a number of skilled 'beetlers' taken across from the north of Ireland.

Glasgow.
On the Clyde.

99. This glorious card, published by Stewart and Woolf of London and printed in Bavaria, was posted in Falkirk on 11 February 1910 to an address in Maryhill. The written message ends 'with the same old fond loving heart. I close. Violet'. The postcard is delicately tinted in silvery grey for the river, black for the shipping and the buildings, orange for the sky which has golden clouds, and a puff of silver smoke is rising from the funnel on the left. The overall effect is quite marvellous, even if the Clyde has scarcely ever looked quite like that!

100. This view of the Clyde at Govan was taken about 1905. Note the 'Cumberland' moored on the right and the industrial landscape of tall chimneys behind the passing steamer on the left. Shipbuilding was a major source of employment and the number of men and boys directly occupied in Glasgow, Govan and Partick in 1901 included ship platers and riveteers 824, 1,745 and 1,038; other workers in iron 292, 256 and 176; shipwrights 456, 1,085 and 590; other workers in wood 102, 247 and 205; others in ship-boat building 1,336, 1,997 and 1,605 (figures for Glasgow, Govan and Partick respectively). In all 61 females, all but 1 in the last occupational category, also worked in shipbuilding.

Govan Ferry

101. This card by Valentine, undated but perhaps about 1905, shows one of the older sites of ferries across the Clyde at Govan. The ferry vehicle details are interesting. Note the two boilers, the areas for carts, waggons, and other transport on either side (there is a cab with horse on the left here), and the platforms at each end. The photograph gives an impression of a hive of activity in the yards and wharfs behind. The ferrymen may have been included in the 93 men (also 2 women) listed in the 1901 Census as bargemen, lightermen and watermen in Glasgow, or in the 64 living in Govan or the 3 in Partick. The Census also lists 147, 22 and 22 men (and 4 women) for Glasgow, Govan and Partick as engaged in the navigation service on shore.

ON THE CLYDE, GLASGOW.

102. This Art Publishing Company card of a packed River Clyde is undated. The importance of the river and the sea for Glasgow is perhaps indicated by the number of men and boys employed in the Merchant Service as seamen, pilots and boatmen in 1901. In Glasgow this was 3,577, and in Govan and Partick 902 and 221 (also 36 females in all). In addition there were 2,851 men working as dock labourers and wharf labourers in Glasgow (and 1 woman), and in Govan and Partick 982 and 73; and 91, 69 and 6 men as harbour, dock, wharf and lighthouse officials in Glasgow, Govan and Partick.

Clyde from Sailors Home, Glasgow.

103. This undivided back Reliable Series card was posted in Glasgow on 24 January 1903. It is greatly enhanced by the crammed message round the photograph in tremendously neat handwriting. The view of the Broomielaw shows four Clyde steamers on the south bank and five steamers on the north bank on the left, perhaps thought off primarily as used for holiday runs but also, of course, essential lifelines for goods and commerce to the island and coastal communities in the west of Scotland. International and local trade and commerce provided a great deal of employment with 1,738 men employed as warehousemen in Glasgow, 53 in Govan and 49 in Partick (and 682, 60 and 7 women as warehousemen).

104. This card is from a superb Art Publishing Company Fresh Air Fortnight Series immortalising the traditional Doon th' Watter holiday for Glasgow families. Enormous crowds went on day trips from the Broomielaw down the Clyde, but for the annual week or fortnight holiday families often took houses or but and ben cottages or apartments in perhaps a Rothesay tenement. Here pa, ma, the weans and the parrot make their way from their close in style to the Broomielaw. Note the cab number (170), the luggage and costume details, and the lively dialogue. 'Fou' implies a degree of alcoholic intoxication. Cards 104 and 108 were sent to Miss Toward at 114 North Street, and are from the National Trust for Scotland's Toward Collection.

105. This photograph of the Broomielaw about 1902 is taken looking towards (rather than from) the Caledonian Railway Bridge. The steamer here is the 'Madge Wildfire', built in 1886 in Ayr, not broken up until 1945, and when this photograph was taken one of the Caledonian Steam Packet Co. vessels. It was probably setting off for Gourock, Kilcreggan and Cove. Note the densely packed little Clutha No. 4 waterbus on the right. This is not high summer traffic yet here, but perhaps rather more typical of June or September when there was still a steady stream of passengers rather than the thousands each day of July and August. Only the rich, remember, went abroad!

Bridge Wharf, *Glasgow.*

106. This card, published by Chas. L. Reis and Co., was posted in Glasgow on 19 August 1914. This view, described as Bridge Wharf, Glasgow, was then perhaps taken on one of the last of the truly golden days before the Great War began to devastate the old Europe. Chas. L. Reis of 49 Jamaica Street was a jeweller and watch and clock importer, with premises also at 50 and 209-215 Argyle Street and 2-4 Jamaica Street in Glasgow, at 115 Grafton Street and 10 and 11 Lower Sackville Street in Dublin, and at 28 Castle Place and 51 Donegal Place in Belfast.

107. This Doon th' Watter summer morning scene, taken at 11.25 a.m., shows the 'Minerva' at Princes Pier, Greenock about 1902. The 'Minerva', built at Clydebank in 1893, was a Glasgow and South Western Railway Company steamer. She is probably here en route to the Kyles of Bute and Rothesay.

108. This second Art Publishing Company Fresh Air Fortnight postcard is perhaps one of the most informative Doon th' Watter cards. The cottage with the thatched roof is clearly the one the family hope to rent, but they are fairly staggered at the exorbitant rent suggested of £10 a month. The proprietor or landlady has that air of moral rectitude and complacent self-satisfaction that only the knowledge that there is no alternative on the island can bring. The day trippers on the steamer are getting only 30 minutes on shore. And the parrot has the last word on the matter!

109. The phrase in 108 'We'll sleep under a boat maw' recalls the remarkable (although later) 'Suzie's Castle' at Portincaple on the shore of Loch Long. The 'castle' was the upturned fishing boat where old Susie lived. She was also an occasional washerwoman and fishwife selling the fish caught up her husband 'Jimmie the Rhu', who was a hand-line fisherman. Susie also sold postcards of her castle and herself and her cats (by repute 13 of them) and 'natural' spring water at 2d for a tumbler.

110. This photograph around 1905 of the Royal Mail Steamer 'Columba' is by Adamson and Son of Rothesay. The 'Columba', built at Clydebank in 1878 and broken up in 1936, was one of the David Macbrayne fleet, and a most beautiful sight she must have been with her elegant long lines, Macbrayne colours, and large funnels. The 'Columba' did the long run to Ardrishaig. 301 feet long and accommodating 2,000 passengers, yet only 9 feet in draught, she took the distances in her stride at by modern standards of Clyde cruising quite amazing speeds.

111. It is very easy to make this world of Edwardian cruising sound like a perpetually idyllic existence. The reality could be very different, as the steamers in general had only rather spartan facilities in rough weather. This Miller and Lang National Series card, posted on 24 August 1905, is the perfect remedy for any too innocent view of days and nights Doon th' Watter. Note the functional quality of the utensils.

I bought this card in Musselburgh. Thanks for letter postcard.

(new in the paper that in Paris it has been much colder than in Edinburgh. Lowest temperature Paris 19°. London 30°. Edinburgh .)

The glass as shown warned the weather yesterday it did not freeze.

CLYDE STEAMERS, "QUEEN ALEXANDRA".

This is a turbine steamer which goes from Glasgow to Greenock and across the Clyde to the islands.

112. The 'Queen Alexandra', built in 1902, was one of the Williamson steamers (white funnels with black tops) owned by Turbine Steamers Ltd. She is probably here en route from Greenock to Campbeltown. The card is one of the Wrench Series, printed in Saxony, and posted in Musselburgh on 3 March 1903. The writer uses both the divided back and the margins round the photograph; the comments are very detailed and suggest that he was interested in meteorology and in steamers.

FAIR AT BRODICK, ARRAN. 10,476. G.W.W.

113. This extremely detailed George Washington Wilson photograph, taken around 1890, shows two paddle-steamers at Brodick on Arran. Most Brodick views show only the Pier itself and the mountains beyond, but the most important aspect of this study is the immense amount of information that can be gleaned about the fair in the foreground, with its shooting galleries and Aunt Sallies and tip-the-lady-out-of-the-bed stalls. Note also the cattle, the people having a picnic on the beach, and the crowd at the end of the pier.

114. The 'Columba' is seen here around 1905 at Ardrishaig on Loch Fyne at the end of its 90 mile run from Glasgow. The splendid David Macbrayne 'Summer Time' guide shows that the 'Columba' or the 'Iona' sailed daily (Sundays excepted) from Glasgow at 7. a.m., Greenock 8.40 a.m., Gourock 9.15 a.m., Dunoon 9.30 a.m., and then, with stops at Rothesay, Colintraive, Tighnabruaich, Tarbert Outer Pier, to Ardrishaig. *At Ardrishaig passengers for Oban and the North land and proceed without delay to the Canal steamer 'Linnet'. Those passengers who have got their baggage properly labelled for the pier in the North at which they intend to land, need not trouble about seeing it forwarded, as this is done for them. The 'Columba' returns from Ardrishaig about 1 p.m. on the arrival of the passengers from Oban and the North.*

STEAMER & COACHES, TROSSACHS PIER.

115. Another popular day out from Glasgow was to explore the Trossachs area. This Caledonia Series card by W. Ritchie and Sons, pencil dated August 1913, shows Trossachs Pier on Loch Katrine with a steamer, probably the 'Sir Walter Scott', at the far end. The four horse-drawn vehicles are occupied by extemely affluent looking ladies and gentlemen. Note the white bearded and the grey bearded local men on opposite sides of the horse team on the right. The white beard is giving the photographer a none-too-friendly look as much as to suggest that he is taking far too long a time fussing over his work and keeping the drivers and passengers waiting.

116. This is a marvellous crowd scene — amazing excitement and confusion as a motley assortment of ladies and gentlemen (in a huge variety of hats of all sorts and shapes and sizes) attempt to board the S.S. 'Kinloch' at Campbeltown around 1910. The 'Kinloch', built in Glasgow in 1878 for the Campbeltown and Glasgow Steam Packet Company, did the run from Greenock to Campbeltown. Note the uniforms (at least five, possibly of members of a militia unit?) and the member of the crew at the gangway (wearing a bow tie).

117. This T. and R. Annan and Sons photograph of a Fair Saturday crowd at 10.16 a.m. at Glasgow Central Station is another superb congested scene about 1908. The railway companies, of course, were at least as busy as the Clyde steamship companies and probably carried many more passengers on holidays. The advertisements include 'Don't Worry Try Sunlight Soap', 'Haig's Glen Leven The Whisky', 'Venus Soap', 'Van Houten's Cocoa', 'Corry and Cos Aerated Waters', and 'Pattison's Pale Ale'. Note the bookstall, the clock, and the steam trains at platform 4.

118. This Miller and Lang National Series card about 1905 is another from the 'In the Good Old Summer Time' series. It sums up the delights of Third Class travel quite delightfully. As the laddie on the right is saying 'We're a gaun doon th' watter', but in this instance by train to Troon or Prestwick or Largs, or possibly to Gourock for a sail to Dunoon. Note the neat little sketch of 'Old Squiffy', the guard, who clearly has heard somewhere that Glasgow S'Miles Better!

Glasgow Exhibition. Bungalow Restaurant and University in Back Ground.

119. The 1901 International Exhibition at Kelvingrove Park was an enormous success, with over 11 million visitors, and was a perfect expression of the status of Glasgow as an imperial city, the Second City of Empire. Everything was on a larger scale, including the Industrial Hall covering 6 acres and the Machinery Hall covering 5 acres and filled with locomotives and engines and machines. The Bungalow Restaurant with its echoes of the Indian Empire makes an amusing contrast with the Gothicity of the University building behind. Postcard coverage was extensive and it seems likely that T. and R. Annan and Sons, who were commissioned as official photographers for the Exhibition, provided most of the photographs used in the cards sold at the Exhibition. (The 1911 Exhibition was rather different in this respect as the postcard market was much larger and more open to competition.)

Glasgow Exhibition.   Russian Section.

120. The contribution made by the Russian Empire at the 1901 Exhibition was very extensive, indeed it was so large, possibly because of the personal interest of the Tsar, that their section opened weeks after the Exhibition itself had begun. The seven buildings, including four pavilions, had huge displays covering the minerals and forestry and agriculture of Imperial Russia, which of course included then Finland, Estonia, Latvia, Lithuania, and much of Poland. The card gives a good idea of the scale of their section. Note also the very affluent looking visitors in the foreground.

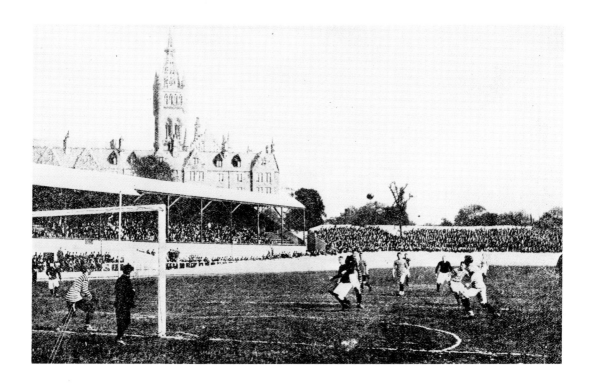

121. The Charity Cup Tie on 4 May 1901 at the Exhibition Stadium (with the University of Glasgow looking on) was a match played between Queen's Park (in black and white hooped jerseys and white shorts) and Third Lanark (in scarlet jerseys and white shorts). Third Lanark, whose original colours were scarlet jerseys, blue knickerbockers and blue stockings, had some considerable successes in this turn of the century period, winning the Scottish Cup in 1899 and 1905, the Scottish League in 1903-04, and the Glasgow Charity Cup of 1900-01 by beating Celtic in the final at the Exhibition Stadium. Note that the Queen's Park goalie is also wearing a black and white hooped jersey.

122. The 1901 Exhibition Sports included the Merchants Charity Cup 10 Miles Scratch Race on 18 May. This view of the carefully controlled and assisted start of the race, with a large crowd watching, is another photograph showing the success of the events and activities provided and the imagination of the organisers in presenting a mixed and varied programme designed to appeal to all sections of the community in the West of Scotland. Indeed the record of the Exhibition is a gallery of popular culture. It was also, like the Los Angeles Olympics, a profit-making enterprise, just as the 1888 Exhibition, which had produced a surplus to help to finance the building of the Kelvingrove Art Gallery in time for the 1901 Exhibition, had likewise been a viable exercise.

123. The 1901 Exhibition was good 'show business' with concerts and performances from orchestras and military bands from Germany, Austria-Hungary, Romania and France. This remarkable picture shows Herr Moser's Berlin orchestra at its Farewell Concert on 22 June. Perhaps a more than mildly amusing example of true grit and the human capacity for suffering for the sake of culture, it must also have gladdened the hearts of musical instrument makers (244 men and 6 women in Glasgow in 1901) and umbrella, parasol and stick manufacturers and workers (205 men and 464 women in Glasgow in 1901) to see such dedication and good sense applied to the use of their respective products. The photograph perhaps helps to explain why Glasgow is the cultural capital of Scotland!

124. The most surprising postcard of the 1901 International Exhibition, however, is this one featuring Charles Rennie Mackintosh's Competititon Design for a Building for a Concert Hall, even if it does look rather like an Edward VII muffin dish. Mackintosh (1868-1928) was then in the middle of his most successful period in Glasgow and had been acquiring a reputation as far away as Berlin and Vienna, so it is very appropriate to find his work featured here.

Scottish Historical (1911) Exhibition. A Glimpse of Old Glasgow.

125. The aims of the also highly successful 1911 Scottish Exhibition of National History, Art and Industry were, as the title indicates, quite different from those of 1901. Although it had some exotica, for example an 'African village', it was an intensely Scottish experience for visitors, all carefully recorded in scores if not hundreds of different postcards. This Miller and Lang National Series card was posted on 1 July 1911. The figures at the front, included a ghostly looking piper, have been almost certainly added to the photograph (however parapsychologists are free to differ in their interpretation!). The architecture of 'Old Glasgow' is a carefully composed series of buildings derived from studying old prints and photographs of the High Street and area.

6368—11

ENTRANCE TO OLD SCOTTISH VILLAGE.
THE SCOTTISH NATIONAL EXHIBITION, GLASGOW.

126. With so many able architects and so much fine Victorian and Edwardian architecture in Glasgow it is not really surprising to find that the 1911 Exhibition had many scholarly reconstructions of old buildings. The 'Old Scottish Village and Town', set sometime in the late seventeenth or early eighteenth century and seen here outside the entrance beyond a charming little toll house, featured carefully constructed replicas in the Scottish vernacular tradition of a tower-house, an inn, a market cross, shops and booths, and various examples of domestic architecture with crow-stepped gables abounding. Note the University tower behind. Compare National Trust for Scotland restoration and rebuilding work in the Lothians and Fife over the last fifty years.

THE MOUNTAIN RAILWAY.
THE SCOTTISH NATIONAL EXHIBITION, GLASGOW

6368 28

127. This Rotary Photographic Series card of the Great Mountain Scenic Railway (fare 6d) highlights the verve and imagination of the organisers of the 1911 Exhibition, for this is a real fun piece. What could have been more suitable and attractive in Glasgow, a city from where railway locomotives were exported all over the world, than a novelty 'railway'? In the photograph the scene takes on something of the nature of an almost lunar landscape, but this may just be the distorting image the camera sometimes produces. Note again the crowds and queues.

An Rathad Mor a' Chlachain – The Chlachan High Street.   C 103

128. Undoubtedly the most photographed of all the attractions at the 1911 Exhibiton was the remarkable Clachan – or, to give it its proper title, 'An Clachan The Highland Village'. It was entered through a quite extraordinarily unsuitable gateway with pepperpot turrets, the sort of object a successful sausage manufacturer might have put up at his Highland shooting lodge. The Clachan came complete with Post Office and book shop (!) and 'High Street' (An Rathad Mor a' Clach Ain). This card, printed for Alexander McLaren and Son, An Clachan Post Office and 360 Argyle Street, Glasgow, was posted on 31 July 1911.

The Clachan.
The Scottish National Exhibition.

129. This Art Publishing Company card was posted on 2 July 1911 to Mrs. McIntyre of Leith 'from Myself'. In both 128 and 129 the architectural detail is good, the thatched roofing, the stone and straw chimneys, the stony pathway, the peat stack all suggest careful thought and planning. The overall layout, however, is another matter, and whether there was ever a 'clachan' that looked like this one is open to doubt. The overall effect is the problem rather than the individual buildings, which would fit happily enough into a modern 'folk museum' complex.

6368—17

THE HIGHLAND CLACHAN.
THE SCOTTISH NATIONAL EXHIBITION. GLASGOW.

130. This Rotary Photographic Series card was posted on 22 May 1911 at the Clachan Post Office with the official postmark to the left of the Glasgow franking. The cottage detail, including the thatching, is good. Unfortunately doubts begin to creep in when the 'cast' is examined. The genuine 'Highlander' is the thin man on the left in the dark clothes, who could easily be a keeper or a crofter fisherman; the dazzling figure on the right with medals, sporran, buckled shoes and fancy stockings is the synthetic version with more than a touch of the 'Brigadoons' about him.

131. This very fine T. and R. Annan and Sons photograph of the assembled 'cast' at the Clachan shows in detail the amazing hotch-potch of costumes ranging from the incredible to the merely picturesque. Exceptions are the older woman third from the right at the front and the woman in the dark checked dress second to her left who do look 'authentic', that is they look like the sort of people one might expect to meet in a real clachan. The four young ladies in cream or white dresses sitting on the grass seem quite out-of-place. The male attire bears little relationship to anything likely to be seen in a clachan then or during the previous century.

"OH. ARE YE SLEEPIN' MAGGIE"

132. The hordes of humourous cards published by Miller and Lang and the Art Publishing Company are, even if there is no evidence of a Lavery or a Henry at work, usually beautifully drawn and coloured and generally sweetly witty rather than coarse. They are important evidence of generally held attitudes and opinions and also a means of reinforcing or even forming attitudes. This Miller and Lang card is a good antidote to the romantically false or inadequate stereotypes in 128 to 131. The winter scene is good again on architectural detail and the costume detail a good deal more 'authentic'. Film buffs will remember some of the 'Lassie' films here!

133. This Miller and Lang National Series undivided back card was posted on 29 September 1903. Glasgow was the main 'joke factory' for the exuberant Scotch humour of the period. And perhaps because the Scots were so successfully part of a great Empire and because their working population employed in heavy industry were among the best paid in the world, they were able to laugh unselfconsciously at images of the 'truly unspeakable Scot'. In this 'nicht wi' Burns' card the mini kilts, more 'authentic' just because they are so short, are in a plain reddish orange tartan, nicely matching the noses of the wearers.

134. Above: this 'La Tartantelle' undivided back card, published by W. Ralston, the photographer, of 259 Sauchiehall Street, was posted on 2 August 1903. The costume detail is rather super, with the 'boy' on the left bearing a remarkable and hardly coincidental resemblance to BPC (Bonnie Prince Charlie). The boy and the girl are in Macleod Dress tartan in yellow, red and black. He has yellow, red and black check stockings and she has plain black stockings. The magnificent and quite unwieldy sporran adds the final touch to this charming little skit.

Below: the beautifully drawn Art Publishing Company card was posted in Kirkcudbright on 1 October 1904. The thistle man is tinted in purple and green and the two Scottish gentlemen are in grey and blue grey. This will evoke an immediate response from anyone who has had the misfortune and the dreadful embarrassment of travelling inadvertently on a train from Glasgow to London within two or three days of an England versus Scotland football match at Wembley. The prickly Scot is a stereotype all too accurately presented here.

135. Above: this card is not on a par with the work in most Miller and Lang and Art Publishing Company cards, but it is interesting as an example of a signed card published by the Newman Brothers of Glasgow, printed in Holland, and posted in Paisley on 27 April 1912. In those happy and secure days when ministers in the Established Church were generally highly respected for their moral integrity, it was possible and indeed commonplace to poke fun at them just because their honesty was accepted without question. The 'bang goes sixpence' type of joke was also, of course, a very general theme in Scotch cards.

Below: the Miller and Lang National Series card was posted in Glasgow on 19 July 1904. The members of these Scottish regiments (perhaps Territorials?) on a summer camp exercise look as if they are rehearsing for a 1980s style television commercial. If regulars they might have been among the 482 military personnel stationed at Maryhill Barracks in 1901 (with 75 male servants and non-military personnel and 144 females). In Glasgow as a whole, including Maryhill, there were 31 army officers and 751 soldiers and non-commissioned officers in 1901, and 1,373 policemen.

"ONE SABBATH IN A SCOTTISH LANE, WHILST HOME FROM KIRK WAS WENDING MAC SAW A SAXPENCE ON THE GROUND, BUT THE MINISTER CAUGHT HIM BENDING!"

ON CANTEEN DUTY

"HAME CAM' OOR

GUIDMAN AT E'EN."

National Series

M. & L.,
C.

136. This Miller and Lang National Series card was posted on 13 August 1903 to a lady near 'Berriedale, Caithness, N.B.' – 'Have you got that salmon yet?' Using animals to point moral lessons was a popular device in postcard art, just as in mediaeval illuminated manuscripts. 'Scotch Cats' or 'Alcoholism to an Extent' would be good titles for this card, but the 'Hame Cam' Oor Guidman at E'En' fits in very well with Mrs. Cat ready with her welcoming poker. The whisky is 'Old H.'. (N.B.: of course, refers to 'North Britain'.)

137. This card, published by E.W.T. Dennis and Sons, was posted at Kilmun on 21 July 1911. Although gentle humour compared with the frightening Florence Upton 'Golliwogg' cards published by Tuck post 1903, nevertheless the racialist implications are clear. Little Black Sambos were more general on cards than even Wee Macgreegors. No malice was intended, but it was part of an overall assumption of condescending superiority towards the 'lesser races' quite as common in Scotland as in England. Words and phrases used in the 1900s have often quite different meanings in the 1980s: an obvious example is the hugely sentimental Lauder song 'When I get back to Bonnie Scotland' in which he refers to being away for seven years 'fighting niggers'.

SUNRISE AT KILMUN.

QUEEN ALEXANDRA

138. Given Kilmun's location on the Holy Loch, which has more Soviet nuclear missiles targeted on it than any other site possibly in Europe, perhaps 137 should have been given the title 'Sunset at Kilmun' or 'The Last Sunset'. However these cards were produced in the optimistic Edwardian world, and it is more appropriate to end with this charming Art Publishing Company card posted in Glasgow on 24 April 1905. The Clyde steamer is again the 'Queen Alexandra', as in 112. The moonlight effect is, of course, a fake, but it is a very successful piece and the silhouette of the figures on the right is, to use a very Glasgow word, 'magic', so that overall it is a wee stunner!